JON KRAKAUER

CLASSIC KRAKAUER

Jon Krakauer is the author of eight books and has received an Academy Award in Literature from the American Academy of Arts and Letters. According to the award citation, "Krakauer combines the tenacity and courage of the finest tradition of investigative journalism with the stylish subtlety and profound insight of the born writer."

www.jonkrakauer.com

CLASSIC KRAKAUER

CLASSIC KRAKAUER

Essays on Wilderness and Risk

JON KRAKAUER

ANCHOR BOOKS
A Division of Penguin Random House LLC
New York

The pieces first appeared in the following publications:
Medium: "Embrace the Misery" (July 29, 2014)
New Age Journal: "A Clean, Well-Lighted Place" (December 1985)
The New Yorker: "Death and Anger on Everest" (April 21, 2014)
Outside: "After the Fall" (June 1990),
"Fred Beckey Is Still on the Loose" (July 1992), "Loving Them to Death" (October 1995), "Mark Foo's Last Ride" (May 1995)
Smithsonian: "Gates of the Arctic" (June 1995),
"Living Under the Volcano" (July 1996)
Smithsonian Air & Space: "Descent to Mars" (November 1995)

Library of Congress Cataloging-in-Publication Data
Names: Krakauer, Jon, author.
Title: Classic Krakauer : essays on wilderness and risk / by Jon Krakauer.
Description: First Anchor Books edition. | New York : Anchor Books, a division of Penguin Random House LLC, 2019.
Identifiers: LCCN 2019018697 (print) | LCCN 2019021956 (ebook) |
ISBN 9780525562733 (ebook) | ISBN 9781984897695 (paperback : alk. paper)
Subjects: LCSH: American essays. | Wayfaring life.
Classification: LCC PS3561.R238 (ebook) | LCC PS3561.R238 A6 2019 (print) |
DDC 814/.54—dc23
LC record available at https://lccn.loc.gov/2019018697

Anchor Books Trade Paperback ISBN: 978-1-9848-9769-5
eBook ISBN: 978-0-525-56273-3

Book design by Steven Walker

www.anchorbooks.com

Printed in the United States of America
10   9   8   7   6   5   4   3   2   1

For Linda

CONTENTS

CLASSIC KRAKAUER

INTRODUCTION

I embarked on a literary career in the early 1980s by writing freelance magazine articles for *Outside, Rolling Stone, Smithsonian*, and a motley of lesser-known publications. To make rent, I had to hustle thirty or forty assignments per year, and most of what I wrote was garbage. But I managed to scrape together a meager living, and learned my craft in the bargain. In 1990, a small independent publisher collected a dozen short pieces I'd written about climbing and published them as a book called *Eiger Dreams: Ventures Among Men and Mountains*, for which they paid me an advance of $2,000. I was ecstatic.

This princely sum wasn't enough to keep the creditors at bay, however, so I continued to crank out magazine pieces at a frenetic pace, one of which I expanded into a second book, *Into the Wild*, published in January 1996. After my third book, *Into Thin Air*, was released fifteen months later, I had the financial means to cut back drastically on magazine work and pursue book-length projects instead. It was liberating to be able to focus on a single undertaking for five or six years, instead of juggling multiple assignments that had to be completed in a matter of months, if not weeks, to ward off financial disaster.

Most of the short pieces I wrote during the years between *Eiger Dreams* and *Into Thin Air* vanished into the crevices of time and have been forgotten. But Anchor Books has retrieved eight articles from this period, plus two more recent essays, and rescued them from oblivion with this new collection, *Classic Krakauer: Essays on Wilderness and Risk*. Thanks for giving it a look.

MARK FOO'S LAST RIDE

Twenty-two miles down Highway 1 from San Francisco, a craggy fist of land called Pillar Point thrusts emphatically into the cold Pacific. Friday, December 23, 1994, dawned fair over this stretch of coast. Mountainous waves crashed against the headlands, spraying up billows of mist that unfurled languidly across the beaches. Beyond the end of the point, some fifteen surfers bobbed in the winter sunlight, scanning the horizon for approaching swells.

It was not uncommon to see surfers off the point—a spot they called Mavericks—dressed in heavy, hooded wetsuits and sitting astride oversize boards. But the hovering helicopter, the three boats of photographers just outside the surf line, and the throng of spectators lining the cliffs suggested this was no ordinary surf session.

For more than a week, the largest, most perfectly shaped waves in a decade had been thundering over the reef at the end of Pillar Point. Word traveled quickly over the international surfers' grapevine: Mavericks, which had recently emerged as one of the world's heaviest waves, was going off. Upon hearing the news, a trio of renowned big-wave surfers from the Hawaiian Islands—Brock Little, Ken Bradshaw, and Mark Foo—hurried to California to join the local crew in the surf.

The names and faces of the three Hawaiians were familiar to most of the five million surfers on the planet. Who among them was top dog in the surf was a matter of lively debate, but there was no disagreement over who cut the highest profile out of the water.

Mark Sheldon Foo was not afflicted with an excess of modesty or self-doubt. In his résumé, he unabashedly described himself as "surfing's consummate living legend." Detractors called him grandiose, and worse, but it didn't crimp Foo's style. In his Filofax were the phone numbers of surfing's premier photographers, whom he cultivated and kept in close contact with. His picture appeared in print with uncanny frequency, and he hosted a surfing show on cable television.

Foo made no bones about his thirst for fame or his strategy for achieving it: ride the world's biggest waves with singular audacity and do it when the cameras were rolling. That Friday morning, cameras were present in abundance to document the historic convergence of Foo and his celebrated colleagues on Mavericks. It promised to be a momentous coming out for an underappreciated California wave.

Despite its proximity to San Francisco and Santa Cruz, as recently as 1990, only a handful of locals had ever heard of Mavericks, and only one brave soul—a townie named Jeff Clark—had actually surfed it. By and by, rumors started to drift up the coast about a mysto surf break near Half Moon Bay that generated thick, grinding barrels tall enough to drive a bus through. They were reputed to be at least as big as—and considerably more hollow than—the famous waves that rumbled ashore at Hawaii's Waimea Bay, the Mount Everest of surfing. Mavericks, moreover, gave off a vibe that made Waimea's daunting aura seem benign by comparison. A 1992 article by Ben Marcus in *Surfer* magazine described Mavericks as "gloomy, isolated, inherently evil. The reef is surrounded by deep water, and lies naked to every nasty thing above and below the Pacific: Aleutian swells, northwest winds, southeast storms, frigid currents, aggro elephant seals and wilder things that snack on aggro elephant seals." Taped to the wall of a bait shop at Pillar Point Harbor is a faded newspaper clipping about a local fisherman who pulled three great white sharks from the surrounding waters in a single day.

Initially, as luck would have it, the waves that Friday morning failed to live up to the inflated expectations of the visiting surfers and assembled media. As they paddled out to the lineup, none of the Waimea veterans was especially impressed or intimidated by what he saw. The epic surf of the preceding week had diminished somewhat. The crowds in the water and on the cliffs provided an uncharacteristic sense of security. "It was a little anticlimactic," Bradshaw confirms. "A few big sets came through, but nothing really huge. Everybody was just out there having fun."

Shortly before noon, however, Mavericks showed its true face. Somebody in the gallery on the cliffs yelled, "Set!" A procession of telltale black lines was rushing toward the point at 22 knots. Half a mile offshore, Bradshaw saw the approaching swells and maneuvered into position.

He let the first wave of the set roll under him, then started paddling in earnest for the next one. As the swell charged out of deep water and rushed over the reef, it humped up to the dimensions of a drive-in movie screen, seemed to pause for a beat to marshal its power, and began to topple forward. Digging hard down the surging face, Bradshaw noticed Foo— his friend, his longtime antagonist—several yards ahead and slightly to the right, scrambling for the same wave.

According to the unwritten rules of surfing, the wave belonged to Bradshaw, because he was "deeper"—that is, he was positioned closer to its peak, the part of the wave that would momentarily pitch shoreward and slam down. "But I was maybe a little too deep," Bradshaw reflects, "and I could see that Mark was already committed, so I decided to back out and let him have it." Pulling up abruptly, Bradshaw plunged his legs to either side of his board and jammed on the brakes.

The wave bucked to full height and then slid out from under him. Perched for a moment on the tottering, feathering crest, he caught a glimpse of Foo stroking powerfully down the face, ready to leap to his feet, in perfect position to make the wave. The motor drives of more than a dozen cameras, all trained at Foo, began to grind. It was the last time Bradshaw would see Foo alive.

Fairly or not, most of society regards surfing as a summer pastime for feckless adolescents. But big-wave surfing has little in common with fun and games at the beach. The incumbent hazards and challenges lend the activity a seriousness of purpose, a certain nobility, even.

Fewer than a hundred people in the world have the poise and reflexes to drop into the jaws of a 40-foot wave and emerge on their feet. As a wave increases in height, its mass increases exponentially, as does the energy released when it breaks. The difference between riding a head-high wave (the upper limit of most surfers) and riding a hollow, dredging 40-footer is roughly the difference between driving 35 miles per hour and driving 200 miles per hour.

Somewhere between 36 and 40 feet is the size at which big-wave surfing, as Bradshaw puts it, "starts to become real." Not that Bradshaw or any other self-respecting surfer would be caught dead referring to a 36-foot wave as a 36-foot wave. Big-wave surfers employ an arcane calculus of understatement, rigidly adhered to, whereby the height of a wave is pegged at roughly half the actual dimensions of the face. A wave that stands 36 feet from trough to crest is said to be an 18-footer, maybe a 20-footer if the surfer making the assessment is from California rather than Hawaii, and prone to wild exaggeration.

Big-wave surfing originated on the North Shore of Oahu in 1957, when Greg Noll first rode one of the fabled behemoths of Waimea Bay. A handful of others followed suit, and thereafter a fraternity of big-wave enthusiasts coalesced every November with the arrival of the Aleutian juice—potent winter ground swells out of the Gulf of Alaska. For the next twenty-five years, the club remained a tight, self-referential brotherhood, largely uncorrupted by the sporadic attention it received from the world at large. The club's culture was characterized by intense competition and undiluted machismo, but its members, for the most part, were concerned with impressing only one another.

That changed around 1983. The surf was exceptionally large and frequent that winter on the North Shore, and the wealth of astonishing photographs that appeared in the season's wake were widely noticed. After a long preoccupation with squirrelly, small-wave acrobatics and beach-punk attitude, the California-based surf magazines shifted their gaze to the purer, more elemental challenge of giant waves.

As the editorial limelight swung to Waimea and Todos Santos (a lesser big-wave spot off Ensenada, Mexico), corporate America woke up to the marketing potential of big surf. Ad execs discovered that heroic images of men confronting titanic waves could move a lot of product. It became possible for a talented surfer with a modicum of media savvy to earn a modest stipend riding big Waimea.

Coincidentally, 1983 was the year Mark Foo arrived on the scene at the bay. Through a combination of brazen self-promotion and utter fearlessness, he rapidly made a name for himself. Previously, most people rode big waves with a no-nonsense straight-line approach that reduced their chances of wiping out; Foo introduced a flashier style, attacking the giant Waimea waves with the same slashing abandon he demonstrated in small surf. "Mark charged big waves a little harder than most of the other guys out there," says his friend Dennis Pang, a respected North Shore surfer and board builder. "He definitely took bigger risks."

The big-wave brotherhood has always held audacity in high esteem, but a fine distinction is made between boldness and idiocy. The latter is termed *kook behavior* and is one of the worst epithets in the surfers' lexicon. Some of Foo's rivals initially branded him a kook, but his dazzling performance in the water kept the slur from sticking. Before long, indeed, Foo's hairball style informed and inspired a whole new crop of big-wave surfers.

Foo explained the risks he took by saying, "If you want to ride the ultimate wave, you have to be willing to pay the ultimate price." He recited this so often, to so many people, that it became a cliché. But he insisted earnestly to his closest friends that he had a strong feeling he was going to die young. Most of Foo's acquaintances, accustomed to his fondness for melodramatic pronouncements, didn't take him seriously and laughed it off.

A month after Mark Foo's drowning, a few blocks from what passes for downtown Half Moon Bay, Jeff Clark stands in his garage and ponders the tragedy. He, too, was out in the waves that Friday morning, surfing alongside the big-wave elite. On a certain level, as the man who brought Mavericks to the attention of the surfing world, Clark can't help feeling a measure of responsibility for the death of one of his personal heroes.

Ankle-deep in a clean white drift of foam shavings, Clark cuts short his dark ruminations, glances at an order form tacked to the wall, and switches on his electric planer. As he mows broad swaths of polyurethane, the sleek lines of a big-wave board gradually emerge from the crude slab of foam.

In the old days, they were referred to as rhino chasers or elephant guns. Their exaggerated length and spear-like proportions have long provided fodder for parlor analysts. But sometimes—as Freud might have said if he'd surfed instead of smoked cigars—a surfboard is just a surfboard.

Big waves break with formidable speed. In order to catch one—in order to make it down the face ahead of the avalanching lip—a surfer needs a board that can be paddled very fast, which means it must have a very long waterline. The extended length also gives it the requisite stability for negotiating chop at high speed. Nobody in his right mind paddles into 20-foot-plus waves on anything shorter than 9 feet 6 inches.

After roughing out one side of the surfboard, Clark pauses to stare at his half-finished creation, then lays the planer carefully on its side and brushes the foam dust from his arms and shoulders. "You know"—he sighs—"I'm not really into this today. Too many things on my mind. Let's go check out Mavericks."

Clark, thirty-eight years old, is a taciturn, powerfully built man with ice-blue eyes. His unkempt hair is stiff with salt from an early morning surf session. He has lived within five miles of Mavericks since the age of nine.

Hidden behind high bluffs, Mavericks can't be seen from the highway unless you know where to look. It was first noticed in 1962 by a surfer from San Francisco named Alex Matienzo, who paddled out on a small swell and rode some mushy rollers breaking across the inner reef. He named the spot after his German shepherd, Maverick, who followed Matienzo into the waves.

Clark started thinking about surfing Mavericks as a teenager. Every winter he watched meaty, gaping barrels churn past the end of Pillar Point, and wondered why nobody rode them. In the winter of 1974–75 he paddled out alone to have a look, caught five burly waves on a 7-foot-3-inch board (it was the biggest stick he owned at the time), and thereby became the first person to surf Mavericks when it was actually going off.

Unable to convince anyone to join him—the waves were too big, the setting too intimidating—he continued to surf the outside peak by himself for the next fifteen years. Clark was itching to introduce others to Mavericks, to share his discovery, but he didn't mind the solitude. "Spending so much time alone out on the water," Clark says, "I got so I could sense how waves were going to break on a subconscious level." Day by day, year by year, he observed and mentally catalogued every nuance of wind, tide, and swell.

Clark didn't care if the surf was crummy. It didn't matter if he got stuffed by a wave, lost his board, and was forced to make the long swim in. "Tapping into all that power, realizing how small you are," he says, "I get stoked just being out there."

Although he is a surfer of extraordinary talent, Clark never had the chops to make a living on the cutthroat professional contest circuit. Clark admired Foo immensely, in no small part because Foo demonstrated that it was possible to fashion a viable career out of riding big waves. Foo's death—and the fact that he drowned at Mavericks—rocked Clark hard. It was as if Joe Montana had come into his home as a dinner guest, only to choke to death on a chicken bone. "I got there right after they found him," Clark says with a clear, unblinking gaze. "I saw this body in a wetsuit stretched out on the back deck of the boat—it just didn't seem possible that it was Mark."

Climbing the stairs to his cramped second-floor apartment, Clark grabs a pair of binoculars and heads out to the deck. By standing in one corner and leaning over the railing, he can look across the Cabrillo Highway and see a black slice of ocean, drawing an unobstructed bead on Mavericks, five miles up the coast. Squinting through the 10×50 lenses, every few minutes he observes a spume of whitewater erupt high over the sawtoothed cluster of sea stacks at the tip of Pillar Point.

"The swell is coming up," Clark remarks, his voice betraying an uncharacteristic trace of excitement. "Mavericks will probably go off this afternoon on the minus tide."

The outer reef at Mavericks squats 21 feet below the ocean's surface, a mesa of submerged rock sloping abruptly out of deep water. Swells smaller than 10 or 12 feet roll right over the reef without even breaking. But whenever a cell of concentrated low pressure slides down the winter storm track and starts pushing fat, long-interval ground swells ahead of it, Clark keeps his ear glued to his NOAA weather radio for the buoy reports. As the swells come pulsing ashore, the first thing they hit after 2,000 miles of open ocean is Mavericks. Rocketing up the front of the reef like a skier flying off a jump, wave after wave gets launched to astonishing heights.

California is said to be home to more than a million surfers. Why, then, did it take so long for any of them to realize that some of the biggest waves on the planet broke right under their noses? It's not as though Clark tried to keep Mavericks secret. "I wanted someone to surf with," Clark says. "I told a lot of people that Mavericks was a world-class wave, but coming from someone like me it didn't mean anything."

There are some kick-ass surfers in San Francisco, and even more in Santa Cruz, but they were blinded by their provincialism. At the time, it was simply inconceivable to the big dogs of Ocean Beach and Steamer Lane that an unknown surfer from a backwater like Half Moon Bay could have discovered a new wave worthy of their attention.

It wasn't until 1990 that outsiders finally started to sit up and take notice of Mavericks. On January 22, a northwest swell of historic dimensions came ashore up and down the California coast. Jeff Clark had driven into the city to work on a construction project, but when he heard the buoy reports coming over the weather radio, he fled the job site and headed immediately to nearby Ocean Beach. There, in the parking lot, he ran into two well-known Santa Cruz surfers, Dave Schmidt and Tom Powers.

The surf at Ocean Beach had redlined and gone off the scale. Unrideable 30-foot closeout sets were pounding the outer reef with extraordinary violence. Paddling out looked suicidal. Clark told the others that he knew a place where the waves would be even bigger, and perfectly shaped. Powers and Schmidt were skeptical, but followed Clark down to Half Moon Bay.

Clark led them up to a bluff north of Pillar Point and pointed out Mavericks just as a set thundered through. "Dave's jaw dropped," remembers Clark, "and he goes, 'Oh my God! That's Waimea!' Then he starts pacing back and forth, back and forth, looking out at the waves, saying, 'That's huge! I don't believe what I'm seeing! That's Waimea!'" The two newcomers nervously paddled out with Clark. Before the day was over, Schmidt had ridden six waves, Powers caught two, and both men were awed by Clark's performance.

At one point Clark fell as he dropped into a yawning barrel, got crushed by the lip when the wave collapsed, and was held down so long he wondered very seriously if he would have enough breath to make it back to the surface. At the conclusion of the session, everyone was still alive, though, and by the time they left the water, the Santa Cruz surfers were believers.

Over the next two winters, many of the boldest, baddest surfers in California showed up to see if Mavericks was for real. Of those who had also surfed Waimea, most agreed that the California wave broke as big and as thick as anything on the North Shore—and that mistakes at Mavericks are apt to have much more serious consequences. The water is 30 degrees colder than in Hawaii, sapping strength, cramping muscles, significantly reducing the length of time one can hold one's breath. And the necessity of wearing a restrictive, buoyant wet-suit makes it harder to dive under waves in the impact zone.

The scariest thing about Mavericks, though, is the rocks. The outside peak breaks in such a way that any surfer who blows the drop and eats shit early is very likely to get flushed into the boneyard—a jumble of jagged truck-size boulders, against which he will be brutally pounded by each incoming wave.

Clark, who has paid some stiff dues of his own in the bone-yard, says solemnly, "Before you paddle out, you need to think real carefully about the worst-case scenario, and then ask yourself if you're ready to deal with it. Mavericks punishes mistakes more severely than other waves. I've seen some bad things happen out there."

After flying all night from Honolulu, Ken Bradshaw steered the rental car into the rutted beach parking lot at Pillar Point, and he and Mark Foo climbed stiffly out into the morning sun. They were an unlikely looking pair: built like a tight end, with chiseled All-American features, Bradshaw towered over the 5-foot-8-inch Foo, who had the imperturbable face of a Confucian priest. The fact that they had come to Mavericks as close friends was perhaps even more unlikely, given their long and often bitter rivalry.

At thirty-six, Foo was the younger of the two by five years. He still had the taut physique of a flyweight boxer, but the flesh beneath Foo's chin was beginning to slacken, and the skin around his eyes was deeply furrowed. Twenty-six years in the surf was starting to take its toll.

Born in Singapore to parents of Chinese descent, Foo spent most of his childhood in greater Washington, D.C., where his father worked for the U.S. Information Agency. He didn't learn to surf or even swim until the family moved to Hawaii when he was ten, but once introduced to the sport, he resolved to make surfing the whole of his existence.

In 1970, Foo's father was posted back to Washington and the family resettled in suburban Maryland, a move the head-strong twelve-year-old could not abide. Two years after arriv-ing on the East Coast, much to his family's dismay, Foo ran off to Florida to make his mark as a surfer. "Good Chinese boys did not aspire to be surfers," says SharLyn Foo-Wagner, Mark's older sister. "My mother would have preferred he had become a lawyer or a doctor, like our brother, Wayne."

The three Foo children grew up comfortably in a fam-ily whose values were more mainstream American than tra-ditional Chinese, according to SharLyn. "Our dad was your basic Middle American, detached, workaholic father. Our mom was strong-willed, independent, a feminist from way back." Wherever it came from, she says, the Foo kids "were all super intense from an early age."

By the time he was seventeen, Mark had found his way to the North Shore of Oahu, the white-hot nexus of the surfing universe, where he immersed himself in the tournament cir-cuit. Initially, his results were promising, but in 1982, having climbed no higher than 66th in the world professional rank-ings, he was forced to accept that he would never be a star in that arena.

In what proved to be a stroke of brilliance, Foo decided to abandon the pro tour and concentrate instead on getting his image into print, an enterprise for which he turned out to have rare talent. By establishing a close, symbiotic relationship with the top surf photographers, Foo got his picture on the cover of the two major surfing magazines half a dozen times—more often than any of the world champions who'd surfed circles around him on the contest circuit.

His ubiquitous presence in magazines and videos and on television earned him promotional contracts from several surf-related companies, who paid Foo modest sums to be a human billboard for their products. At one point, he even landed a sponsorship deal with Anheuser-Busch, but Foo never got rich. Because he was a freelancer, operating outside the structure of the pro tour, he seldom cleared more than $30,000 annually. But it gave him the means to surf whenever and wherever he wanted, and that was sufficient to win the lasting enmity of envious associates.

Other surfers heaped opprobrium on Foo for his single-minded pursuit of publicity—he didn't surf, they groused, unless the cameras were pointed his way—but he remained remarkably unaffected by the criticism, and continued his quest for surfing glory with unabashed enthusiasm. "Yeah, bruddah Mark loved to have his picture taken," chuckles Dennis Pang, one of Foo's oldest and closest friends. "He caught a lot of shit for it, but it was like water off a duck's back."

In 1983, Foo surfed Waimea Bay for the first time. Unfazed by the bay's mythic reputation, he attacked the enormous waves with a bravado that forced the old guard to take grudging note. In January 1985, Foo took off on a Waimea wave said to be in excess of 60 feet—bigger than anything ever ridden. He dropped off the overhanging ledge, immediately tumbled into the water, and was smothered by the full force of the wave. The impact of the falling lip snapped Foo's board and worked him over like a rag in a wringer, but he popped to the surface unharmed and was quickly plucked from the impact zone by a rescue helicopter.

Even though he hadn't even come close to making the wave, Foo wasted no time in sending accounts of the attempt to magazines around the world, and when these articles were published, they cemented his reputation as a big-wave demigod. In an interview soon thereafter, Foo suggested, "In terms of performance, I don't think anyone surfs Waimea better than I do."

Ken Bradshaw, the reigning king of Waimea at the time, didn't share this opinion. He had been surfing Waimea for nine years before Foo ever dipped a toe in the bay, and the younger surfer's presumptuousness, his braggadocio—his lack of respect—tweaked Bradshaw. Foo lived just down the Kam Highway from Bradshaw, and the two surfers encountered each other often, both in and out of the water. As Foo's meteoric rise continued, those encounters became more and more strained.

The nadir in their relationship occurred in 1987, on the morning of a major surf contest at Sunset Beach. During the warm-up period before competition got under way, according to Pang, "Mark kept dropping in on Bradshaw, stealing his waves, and finally Kenny went ballistic. He went after Mark in the channel and started beating him up, dunking him underwater, holding him down. Ken didn't really hurt Mark, but he embarrassed him in front of all the best surfers in the world. When Mark came in, he called me right away and told me how upsetting it was. He got over it really fast, though. A couple of days later it was like nothing had ever happened. Mark just didn't let that kind of stuff bother him."

A corollary of Foo's unwavering drive was that he was relentlessly, obdurately optimistic. He was convinced it was his destiny to achieve greatness on giant waves. When things got hairy out there, his belief in fate allowed him to maintain a sense of clarity and inner calm. Foo was a religious man; in raging surf—as nowhere else—he felt the rampant presence of the almighty, so close he could taste it in the back of his throat.

Although Foo was monomaniacal and self-absorbed, when it suited him he could be extremely personable, even gregarious. There was something winning about his fervor, his childlike enthusiasm. At least five people considered him their best friend. "You either really liked Mark," says SharLyn, "or you really didn't like Mark. Nobody was indifferent."

For all the derring-do he exhibited in the water, Foo never quite fit the macho cut of the big-wave brotherhood. He was way too willing to discuss his innermost feelings, to bare his emotional underbelly. He wasn't afraid to get touchy-feely. Women fell for Foo hard and often. He showered his sister and mother with earnest, mawkish letters. "Mark and I were so tight," SharLyn acknowledges, "that some people thought we had a kind of weird relationship."

The week before he flew to Mavericks, Foo got engaged to twenty-eight-year-old Lisa Nakano. "He was really in love with Lisa," says Allen Sarlo, one of Foo's closest friends. "And his mom approved of her, which was of major importance to Mark."

Sarlo grows silent for several seconds, then says, "What makes this whole thing kind of heavy is that his older brother, Wayne, died two years ago, just after finishing medical school, and his dad died about three years ago. And recently Mark wrote a letter to his mom telling her that he loved her so much he didn't think he could ever live without her, that he wanted to die before she did. Mark's death has been really devastating to her."

By the time they got their boards out and wetsuits on, it was after nine A.M. when Foo and Bradshaw stroked through the shore break toward the Mavericks lineup. Given the vitriol that had flowed between them over the years, some were taken aback to see the two surfers paddling out together, but their friendship was genuine, insists Dennis Pang: "It wasn't just on the surface. About eight months before Mark died, he and Kenny became real friends."

Last summer Foo explained to a British television crew that he and Bradshaw had "gotten past" their differences, thanks to a bond based on the singular intensity of their shared calling:

"We've experienced things that nobody but he and I have ever done."

Acquaintances credit the rapprochement primarily to the mellowing of Bradshaw. After two decades of proving his mettle at the bay, his place in the hallowed Waimea pantheon was secure. Comfortable in his emerging role as a respected elder of the big-wave fraternity, Bradshaw no longer felt the need to go one-on-one with every swaggering young turk who paddled out. He finally seemed able to accept Foo for who he was, warts and all; Bradshaw found himself reacting with amusement to quirks of Foo's personality that would have triggered apoplectic rage just a few years before.

The previous spring, Foo and Bradshaw had surfed a secret North Shore reef together, a spot called Outside Alligators that Bradshaw discovered and pioneered. "We got some exceptional waves out there," Bradshaw reminisces. "And the place was completely private. Then, after what Mark claimed was maybe the best surf session of his life, he came right in and made, like, thirty phone calls, and suddenly the whole world knew about it. The next time I went out, fifteen guys were there."

"While he was making those calls, I was saying, 'Mark! Put the damn phone down! No one else has to hear about this spot. We can keep enjoying it by ourselves.' But he never saw it like that. He had to share everything with the world." Bradshaw erupts into a deep, ambivalent laugh. "That's just the way Mark was: high-profile all the way."

December 23 marked Foo's first visit to Mavericks, though not Bradshaw's. He'd flown over on several previous occasions, but, he says, "My timing was always a little off. I kept missing the really big days."

Bradshaw had in fact just been to California six days earlier. He spent part of Saturday, December 17, surfing Mavericks in mediocre conditions, then jumped on a plane and flew back to

Hawaii the following morning after hearing that a giant swell was predicted for the North Shore. "Not waiting around a little longer in California was a huge mistake," Bradshaw dolefully concedes. "One of the all-time big mistakes I've ever made."

Even as Bradshaw's jet was hurtling toward Honolulu, an intense 934-millibar low had spun down out of the Gulf of Alaska and stalled off the California coast, commencing a week of the largest, most perfect waves anyone in the state had seen in decades, maybe ever.

"Monday the nineteenth, Mavericks was off the chart," says Mark Renneker, a San Francisco physician who at forty-three is an eminent figure in that city's surfer community. "Wednesday was even bigger."

Jeff Clark, Renneker, a rising star named Evan Slater, a hot Santa Cruz surfer named Peter Mel—everyone present that week knew they were witnessing something momentous. Set after set, somebody would catch the wave of his life. A sixteen-year-old kid from Santa Cruz took off on a wave estimated to be at least 50 feet high, a deed that would put him on the cover of *Surfer*. "Jay Moriarity," the tag line proclaimed, "drops into history at Mavericks."

"When I called Doc Renneker from Oahu and heard what I'd missed," says Bradshaw, "I turned into a basket case." He and Foo jumped on the red-eye and landed in San Francisco as the sun came up Friday morning, hustled out to Mavericks, and were greeted with the news that the surf had gone down overnight. The swell had turned sporadic. Few of the waves were breaking bigger than 25 feet—surf Hawaiians would call 12 to 15 feet.

A big set would steamroll through now and then, however, and the action was pitched among the fifteen surfers jockeying for the waves. The sudden arrival of Foo and Bradshaw cranked up the intensity even higher. "It was a circus out there," says Renneker. "You had these boatloads of photographers, the helicopter, people on the cliffs—and a gaggle of the world's best surfers at Mavericks for the first time. No one had to be told this was a historic day. A good showing in front of all those cameras could make a career. There was incredible pressure to perform."

"The crowd was almost in a frenzy," Clark concurs. "Guys were pushing it maybe a little too far." In the old days, before Foo taught everyone the value of a dramatic photograph, a more conservative attitude prevailed in big waves. Wiping out was considered kook behavior, not to mention dangerous. But the proliferation of sponsorship contracts based on photo incentives changed all that. Because taking off late and deep—down the steepest, most concave part of the wave—creates the most spectacular pictures, ambitious surfers are strongly motivated to hang it out farther and farther, and the consequences be damned.

"As long as you make the drop," muses Bradshaw, "the photographers don't give a shit whether you stay on your feet and actually make the wave. All they want is those three killer shots down the face." That Friday at Mavericks, he says, "Most guys were taking off ridiculously deep for the cameras, and there were some nasty wipeouts as a result."

"I couldn't believe what I was seeing," insists Renneker. "Here were the best big-wave surfers in the world, and they were behaving like fools. Partly it was the fact that some of the guys surfing Mavericks for the first time were underestimating it. Because it was only a California wave, they refused to believe it was as serious as the surf they were used to on the North Shore. But mostly it was just Kodak courage: doing stuff they wouldn't consider doing if the cameras weren't there. And Mark was right in there with them, just as far out of position, making the same mistakes."

Perhaps, Bradshaw concedes. "But what's so strange is that

when Mark took off on the wave that killed him, he was not deep. He was right where he should have been."

Foo had ridden about a dozen waves when, shortly before noon, he saw a beefy set rear up on the horizon. As calculated from photographs, the wave he went for stood approximately 30 feet from trough to crest. Less experienced surfers had ridden larger waves earlier in the week without incident. Foo himself had handled much bigger, gnarlier surf at Waimea on numerous occasions.

He let the first wave of the set go by, then spun around and dug hard for the second. His takeoff looked good. Foo jumped into his trademark crouch as the wave pulled to concave, his arms stretched wide and low for balance. He maintained control when the board went into free fall beneath the overhanging ledge, and seemed to be in equilibrium as he reestablished contact with the wave halfway down the face.

Mavericks, however, is a famously nervous, unpredictable wave. "The bottom configuration, the energy vectors—everything out there is incredibly complex," explains Renneker. "As a consequence, the wave goes through these strange kinks and lifts and drops, all happening in microseconds. You never know what's going to happen next. Mark's surfing reflexes were as good as anybody's in the world, but on some waves there's just nothing you can do to avoid a wipeout."

As Foo angled down the face, observes Allen Sarlo, "the wave jacked and the bottom just fell out of it." Foo's board veered suddenly to the left, the inside rail bogged in some chop, and Foo was thrown violently off the front.

He slammed into the water with tremendous force, a hard belly flop that wrenched his arms back and hyperextended his spine. Foo skipped down the face like a flat stone, and never penetrated the wave far enough to have a shot at escaping out the other side. Embedded in the wall of the heaving green barrel, he was drawn back up the face and sucked over the falls. Viewed in slow motion, the video shows Foo's ghostly silhouette suspended in the roof as the wave throws forward, arches down, and then crashes into the pit with a horrific explosion of whitewater that splintered his board into three pieces.

As Foo had lived, so he died: in the camera's mythologizing eye. More than a hundred people saw Foo get buried by the collapsing lip, and every aspect of the wipeout was captured on film and videotape. Several seconds later, however, Brock Little and Mike Parsons—a renowned big-wave surfer from Orange County who was also surfing Mavericks for the first time that day—took off together on the next wave of the set, and as the immense shimmering wall reared and started to fold over, all eyes turned to watch their ride unfold. Nobody noticed that Foo didn't return to the surface.

As Parsons and Little dropped down the face side by side, the nose of Parsons's board pearled and he went down hard. Two seconds later, Little was mowed, too.

Falling onto his back, Parsons was slammed in the chest by the guillotining lip and driven toward the bottom. "It was maybe the worst wipeout I'd ever had," says Parsons. "It took a really long time to come up. At that point I didn't know the worst was still coming." As he struggled back to the surface, desperate for a lungful of air, he was bumped sharply by what felt like someone's head and arm. At the time, he mistakenly assumed it was Little. It was actually Foo.

Little, by that point, was fighting for his own life about 20 yards away. Caught in the boneyard, pounded repeatedly by incoming waves, both Parsons and Little were swept into the rocks. The leash running from Little's board to his right ankle—a 15-foot polyethylene line strong enough to pull a truck—snagged on a submerged boulder, nearly drowning him, then snapped, and Little was eventually carried through a gap into the safety of the inner lagoon.

Parsons's leash also snagged, but he wasn't so lucky. "I was pinned underwater," he remembers, "getting slammed into a rock by the waves, unable to get a breath. Out of air, I was absolutely sure I was going to drown. I'd written it off and was waiting to die when the wave action suddenly unhooked the leash. I got to the surface, but I took a bad beating before the current finally washed me into the lagoon."

Foo was still nowhere to be seen, meanwhile, and in the excitement over what was happening to Parsons and Little, his absence went unobserved. Bradshaw, outside the surf line, his view blocked by the back of the breaking wave, had no way of knowing that anybody was in trouble. Fifty seconds after backing out of Foo's wave, oblivious to what was happening in the impact zone, Bradshaw took off on the set's last and biggest wave. He nailed the drop, carved hard across the bottom, then charged through the bowl and down the line, covering nearly 300 yards before the whitewater overtook him and knocked him off his board.

Paddling back out to the lineup past the media boats, still buzzing with residual adrenaline, Bradshaw paused to chat with a photographer named Bob Barbour. "Barbour told me that Mark ate it really bad," says Bradshaw, "and that it looked like he'd broken his board. I didn't figure it was a big deal—people break boards all the time. When Mark didn't show up, I just assumed he'd gone in to get another board."

Around one P.M., the sky clouded over and a stiff onshore breeze began to blow, messing up the waves. Surfers started to leave the water, the helicopter departed, the media boats headed in. The *Deeper Blue* started motoring toward the harbor with Parsons, Evan Slater, and two photographers on board. Just beyond the jetty guarding the harbor entrance, somebody noticed the tail block of a purple and yellow surfboard drifting in an eddy. "That looks like Mark's board," Slater casually observed as they cruised past. "Let's go pick it up for him." Then Slater noticed what appeared to be a half-submerged human figure, clad in a black wetsuit, floating face-down beside the broken surfboard. Refusing to believe what they were seeing, someone insisted over and over that it was just a ball of kelp. "No," Parsons replied, feeling dizzy, "that's not kelp." Slater dove in, pulled Foo to the side of the boat, and the others hauled his motionless body onto the back deck.

Until that moment, nobody even suspected Foo was missing. He'd been in the water for more than an hour. The captain immediately radioed the harbor patrol, two paramedics arrived within minutes, but all attempts to revive Foo failed.

Not long thereafter, Bradshaw, one of the last surfers still on the water, caught a final sloppy wave and headed for the beach. In the parking lot, he was approached by Jeff Clark. Stammering, barely able to speak, Clark told him about Foo, and Bradshaw sprinted down to the dock. "I told the sheriff I wanted see Mark," he says, his voice growing thick. "I had to see him with my own eyes to know it was true." Pulling back the blanket that covered the body, Bradshaw looked down at the face of his friend and turned away.

The autopsy determined that the cause of death was saltwater drowning; why Foo drowned remains unclear, however. "It was a heavy wipeout," says Bradshaw, "getting swept over the falls like that, but the same thing has happened a hundred times to all of us."

Foo was found with a small laceration over his right eye and an abrasion across his forehead. Renneker examined the body, however, and he insists that "the head wounds were really very superficial. It's possible that he hit his board and was knocked unconscious, but the pathologist found nothing under the skull to suggest that. My speculation, which is shared by Jeff Clark and others, is that he probably got caught on the bottom."

The ocean floor in the vicinity of Mavericks is riddled with caves, crevices, and sharp, stony projections that bristle like stalks of petrified cauliflower. Foo's body—or his board or his leash—could easily have snagged on some rocky feature that held him underwater, just as Little and Parsons were snagged and held down.

Most of the surfers who were present at Mavericks that day view Foo's death as a freak accident. This may well be the case. But nagging doubts remain.

Much has been made of the fact that death was a subject Foo thought about—and talked about—with great frequency. "Mark often told me that when it was time for him to go, he wanted to die surfing the ultimate wave," says his friend Allen Sarlo. "He told that to everybody. I'd tell him, 'Hey, Mark, you don't have to die to surf the ultimate wave.' But he'd always reply that I didn't understand. He really believed that sooner or later he was going to die surfing."

Foo's friends didn't know what to make of his morbid preoccupation and had trouble reconciling it with the rest of his personality. He didn't exhibit suicidal tendencies and drove his car with the exaggerated caution of an old man. Reckless behavior was anathema to Foo—he almost never drank, didn't even smoke weed. Except for riding big waves, he was loath to engage in hazardous activities of any kind, and the risks he took in the water were very calculated. He spoke enthusiastically to Lisa Nakano, his fiancée, about having children after they were married.

Nakano adds, however, that on numerous occasions Foo mentioned having "this strong feeling he wouldn't live very long. It didn't bum him out or alter the way he conducted his life, but he was convinced he was going to die surfing. He calmly accepted it. At the time, I didn't take him seriously. I don't think anybody did."

Because Foo was in the habit of making overwrought declarations, confirms SharLyn, "most people thought all that stuff about dying was bullshit. Statistically, big-wave surfing just isn't that dangerous."

Rick Grigg fractured his neck at Waimea in 1982. A huge wave snapped Titus Kinimaka's femur there in '89. Foo himself had scars up and down his body from collisions with North Shore coral heads. He shattered an ankle surfing big Pipeline two years ago, and last spring a surfboard fin sliced into his left kneecap, severing tendons and wreaking general havoc. But for all the famous close calls and near-death experiences, Foo was the first expert surfer to die in big waves since 1943. On the face of it, the evidence suggests that surfing giant waves is much less hazardous than climbing, say, or even heli-skiing.

Was it just a fluke, then, that two consecutive waves judged to be of unexceptional size—waves described as 15 to 18 feet by the survivors—killed one of the world's most accomplished surfers, and very nearly killed two others?

The reassuring statistics about the safety of big waves mostly reflect the safety of Waimea Bay, where, until very recently, virtually all big-wave surfing took place. The water there is 82 degrees Fahrenheit, there are no hazards equivalent to the rocks at Mavericks, and the Waimea surf line is patrolled by lifeguards on Jet Skis. A rescue helicopter is on standby.

Mavericks is without question a much more dangerous patch of ocean, and people have been surfing it in significant numbers for less than three years. As more and more surfers visit Mavericks, there will probably be other fatalities, and the statistical likelihood of dying in big waves will have to be adjusted upward.

Not that a murderous reputation is likely to scare elite surfers away. To the contrary, it will probably draw even more of them to Mavericks, just as the malevolent mystique of the Eiger attracts mountaineers in droves. In cultures that idealize boldness—as both climbing and big-wave surfing do—the more dangerous a challenge, the greater the prestige of those who meet it. Nobody understood this better than Foo.

His death is woven through with dark ironies, not least of which is the fact that for years people accused him of overstating the danger of huge surf. But how much was Foo to blame for his own demise? Was he playing too much to the cameras that Friday morning? Did he get careless and make a critical mistake? The answer to both of the latter queries seems to be no. He appeared to be doing everything right on the wave that killed him. Foo, famous for his showboating, was surfing with uncharacteristic prudence when he lost his life.

On December 30, a memorial service attended by 700 people was held on the North Shore of Oahu. More than 150 men and women paddled surfboards into the middle of Waimea Bay to pay their final respects, held hands to form a circle, and cast leis into the sea. Some words were spoken, everyone called out Foo's name thrice, and then Dennis Pang pulled a box of ashes from his backpack and returned Foo to the waves.

After the ceremony, trying to put a positive spin on their loss, several people observed that in making such a theatrical exit at Mavericks, Foo managed to achieve his grandest ambition. In death, he moved beyond mere fame and entered the more enduring sphere of legend. "My bruddah Mark," Pang speculates, "he's sitting up there somewhere, smiling and combing his hair, saying, 'Yeah, top that one!'"

According to SharLyn Foo-Wagner, their mother derives little solace from such thoughts: "My mom is mad. She accepted Mark for what he was, but she never really understood him. It's no comfort to her that Mark was doing what he wanted to be doing when he died. She thinks it's such a waste."

———

At first light on a fogbound California morning, Jeff Clark walks down the beach to the end of Pillar Point and considers the steel-gray expanse of the Pacific. A big west swell is booming over the outer reef, sending mares' tails of spindrift arching high over the barreling waves. Clark zips up his wetsuit, waits for a lull between sets, and starts paddling out. It has been four days since Foo died. Nobody has surfed Mavericks since.

Clark duck-dives under a small inside wave, then catches the outgoing surge and works the rip into the channel. Fifteen minutes later, he's at the lineup. Straddling his board beyond the surf line, for a long time he just stares out to sea, aligning his senses to the ocean's rhythms, trying to sort out the disturbing events of the preceding week—trying, as he would later put it, "to get real clear about Mark's death."

To the west, the surface of the Pacific lifts into a series of sharp black ridges, and the incoming set yanks Clark from his reverie. He lets the first swell roll under him, and the second, then levers his board around and starts to paddle. The sea heaves up beneath him into a towering green peak, vaulting Clark heavenward even as he strokes furiously down the face. As the wave lurches to its apogee, he jumps to his feet and plunges toward the abyss. Above his head, the crest feathers and throws forward into an immense translucent arch.

There are no photographers present, no crowds or boats or helicopters—just Clark, alone, streaking down a colossal wall of salt water. After twenty years, the act still gives him the same pleasure it always has, that shudder of bliss and transcendence. His mind clear and untroubled for the first time in days, Clark accelerates across the trough, leans hard to set the rail, and carves a tight, elegant arc as the wave curls over and tries to swallow him—a roaring, spinning tornado, spewing foam, bearing down fast on his blind side.

LIVING UNDER THE VOLCANO

At 14,410 feet above sea level, I have to pause for breath between each plodding step as I reach the crest of Mount Rainier, the highest point in the Cascade Range. I've climbed this huge volcano many times over the past thirty years—for fun, for exercise, for escape from the urban grind. On this occasion, however, the impetus is morbid curiosity.

Recent geological reports have suggested that Rainier poses a serious threat to thousands of people who live in the shadow of the mountain, as I do, even if it does not erupt. My hope is that this ascent will shed a little light on the matter. Two days of strenuous effort were required to reach the top. Now a surly wind is screaming across the summit crater, flash-freezing the skin on my face and turning my mittened hands into blocks of ice.

Before my eyes is a swath of country that stretches from Canada to central Oregon, some two hundred miles away. Scanning the craggy spine of the Cascades, one can't help noticing that this corner of the planet is lousy with volcanoes: from this lofty vantage, I count no fewer than nine of them. The most riveting—and most notorious—is Mount St. Helens, whose truncated cone squats immediately to the southwest. At the moment, its yawning crater is belching a plume of steam high into the troposphere, a gentle admonition that St. Helens—along with some two dozen other Cascade peaks—is very much an active volcano.

On Sunday, May 18, 1980, shortly before nine o'clock in the morning, I happened to look up from a commercial salmon net I was mending on a dock in Gig Harbor, Washington, and saw what appeared to be a massive cumulonimbus cloud boiling toward the heavens, where a moment earlier there had been nothing but blue sky. Unbeknownst to me, multiple simultaneous avalanches had just carried millions of tons of rock and ice off the top of Mount St. Helens, suddenly removing the geologic lid that had enabled the mountain to contain the molten rock and superheated steam within. The resulting explosion obliterated the upper 1,300 feet of the volcano and sent it hurtling into the sky.

The blast devastated plant and animal life for 150 square miles. The cloud of ash that caught my eye soared to a height of more than 60,000 feet, turning day to night across much of Washington, and scattered 540 million tons of volcanic debris across the western United States. Fifty-seven people were killed, a remarkably small number considering the violence of the eruption. The death toll was so low due to evacuation measures, and because the mountain's rugged environs were sparsely populated and largely undeveloped.

Fifteen years later, as I regard the scenery from atop Mount Rainier, the merest glance between my boots suggests that the consequences could be much more dire when it is this peak's turn to blow. Hard to the northwest sprawl Tacoma, Seattle, and their myriad suburbs. I can plainly make out the Space Needle, skyscrapers in downtown Seattle, and 747s touching down at Sea-Tac Airport.

Given that Rainier has erupted numerous times in the past (most recently, just 150 years ago), the proximity of so much humanity is troubling. Geologists warn that there is no way of knowing when the mountain will blow again—it could go off in ten years or not for ten thousand—but blow it will, eventually.

Hunkered on the crest of Rainier, watching freighters and ferryboats ply the dazzling waters of Puget Sound, it is easy to imagine that the volcano is ready to erupt at any moment. The rim of the summit crater is riddled with fumaroles actively venting hot gases from the bowels of the earth, filling my nostrils with their pungent sulfurous aroma. Even though the air temperature is well below freezing and most of the rest of the mountain wears a carapace of glacial ice hundreds of feet thick, the rocky ground beneath me is utterly bare of snow, and disturbingly warm to the touch. Scientists have recorded surface temperatures on the crater rim as high as 176 degrees Fahrenheit. The heat I feel through my insulated trousers makes it impossible to forget that somewhere not too far below lies a reservoir of fidgety red-hot magma, itching to elbow its way to daylight.

Sixty miles north of Rainier, in a cluttered, windowless room on the University of Washington campus, banks of humming machines keep close tabs on the mountain's every seismological twitch, lest an eruption take the region by surprise. Antennas on the roof of the building gather signals from some thirty remote-sensing devices on or near various Cascade volcanoes: telephones and microwaves carry signals from 120 more. Twelve devices monitor Rainier alone. Tremors large and small show up as squiggly lines on an array of rotating drum graphs in the center of the room.

"Actually," confesses Steve Malone—a cheerful, bearded geophysicist attired in shorts and sandals, who oversees the seismology lab—"the drums provide some useful data, but they are mostly for the benefit of news media. They give TV crews something to point their cameras at whenever there's an earthquake. Here at the lab, we glance at the drums now and then, but mostly we rely on a fairly sophisticated computer system." Should any remote sensor record a seismic event of a magnitude greater than 2.4, the computers are programmed to trigger a beeper that Malone wears on his belt. Additionally, if the event is stronger than 2.9, the system will automatically send out a flurry of faxes and email communiqués to scientists and emergency-management agencies throughout the region.

The big St. Helens blast in 1980 was preceded by a series of minor earthquakes prompted by movement of magma up the throat of the volcano; similar tremors would almost certainly give geologists plenty of notice before Mount Rainier next erupts. "With this system in place," Malone concurs, "the available seismic data should give us warning of an impending eruption weeks or even months in advance."

Truth be told, Malone doesn't think Rainier is a very likely candidate for an explosive St. Helens–like eruption, in any case. Extrapolating from past eruptions, he and most other volcanologists believe that when Rainier blows its lid, it is apt to do so in a much less histrionic fashion, producing relatively modest explosions or extrusions of lava rather than a cataclysmic detonation.

Malone cautions, nevertheless, that it would be a grave mistake to conclude thereby that the mountain presents no great threat: "In fact, Rainier is perhaps far more dangerous than St. Helens. The frightening thing about Rainier is the hazard posed by catastrophic debris flows—a hazard most people aren't even aware of." Known to geologists as lahars (an Indonesian term), such flows are flash floods of semiliquid mud, rock, and ice that surge down from the heights with terrifying speed and destructive power.

"Lahars have occurred throughout Rainier's history," warns Malone, "and they can happen more or less spontaneously, in the complete absence of an eruptive event, with practically no warning at all. Horribly, we remember what happened to Armero, and worry that something similar might happen around here."

Armero was a prosperous farming community nestled in

the Andes in Colombia, not far from Bogotá. On the evening of November 13, 1985, residents of the town felt the earth tremble and heard a series of rumbling explosions emanating from a 17,453-foot volcano called Nevado del Ruiz, thirty miles away. According to a local woman named Marina Franco de Huez, an ominous cloud rose from the mountain's crater, raining ash down on Armero, "but we were told it wasn't anything serious."

Although the volcano was erupting, at first there seemed to be little reason for concern. Indeed, newspaper reports later described the event as a "relatively small eruption, a volcanic burp" that melted only about 5 percent of the ice and snow covering the uppermost reaches of the peak. The "burp" was sufficiently powerful, however, to collapse a steep buttress below the summit crater, initiating an avalanche of rock, snow, and ice—a classic lahar—that swept down the slopes of Nevado del Ruiz from an elevation of 15,000 feet.

Liquefying and gathering momentum as it rocketed down a river drainage toward the valley bottom, the lahar wiped out a natural dam, sending a colossal mudslide downvalley. As one resident of Armero remembered the ensuing cataclysm, "I heard a sound like a huge locomotive going at full steam, and then I felt water swirling around my neck."

Within moments, the town was inundated with a slurry resembling wet concrete, burying the community beneath thirty feet of gray-brown muck. The next morning, where their homes had once stood, survivors gazed upon a stark, lunar-like plain covering 600 acres and littered with smashed cars, corpses, and uprooted trees. An estimated 23,000 people lost their lives, and more than 60,000 were left homeless. It was the worst natural disaster in Colombia's history.

Kevin Scott, a senior geologist at the U.S. Geological Survey's Cascades Volcano Observatory in Vancouver, Washington, warns that there are a number of disquieting parallels between Nevado del Ruiz and Mount Rainier. As he tells me this, he is standing in a field beside a new housing development in Orting, a rapidly growing town in the lowlands near Puget Sound. The Mountain (as Rainier is known locally), gleaming in the summer sun, looms to the southeast less than thirty miles away.

A solitary block of lava as big as a Volkswagen Beetle rests incongruously on a manicured sward behind a recently constructed house. "You know how that boulder got here?" Scott asks. "It was carried down from Rainier by a lahar. This development, like most of the rest of Orting, was built on twenty feet of debris deposited by the Electron Mudflow, a lahar that came down the Puyallup River Valley about five hundred years ago." The geologic record indicates that at least sixty major lahars have roared down from Rainier over the past 10,000 years; a few of them ran all the way to Puget Sound, more than fifty miles from the mountain.

Scott points out that Armero, like Orting, was built on debris from an old lahar: "Armero had already been destroyed at least once, in 1845, before the most recent disaster—by a mudflow that killed hundreds of people. Yet the town was rebuilt in the same place. We can be fairly certain that sooner or later, another lahar is going to plow through Orting, too—we just don't know when.

"Judging from the frequency of mudflows on Rainier in the past, we are reasonably confident that the recurrence interval for major lahars is between five hundred and a thousand years. That sounds like an awfully long time, long enough that we don't really need to worry. Statistically, however, it's been calculated that a house built on the floodplain of a lahar is many times more likely to be destroyed by a lahar than by fire. Almost nobody would consider owning a home without fire insurance and smoke alarms, yet people think nothing of living in the path of mudflows without safeguards. Most folks simply don't take the risk of lahars seriously."

Geologists take lahars very seriously, which is why Mount Rainier makes them so nervous. More than 100,000 people in these environs live in homes built on debris washed down by lahars. Some 200,000 Puget Sound residents go to work each day at businesses lying in the path of documented mudflows. A report published in 1994 by the National Research Council warns, "This metropolitan area is the high-technology industrial center of the Pacific Northwest and one of the commercial aircraft manufacturing centers of the United States. . . . A major volcanic eruption or debris flow could kill thousands of residents and cripple the economy."

Lahars are a hazard of virtually all volcanoes, but Rainier has some unique geologic traits that make it especially dangerous. Thanks to its great height and the sodden Northwest climate, Rainier wears a stupendously robust mantle of ice. Twenty-six named glaciers drape Rainier's broad flanks, a reservoir of snow and ice approximately equal to that of all the other Cascade volcanoes combined. The melting of just a tiny fraction of this frozen water during a volcanic event could unleash lahars of biblical proportions.

"Compared to any other volcano in the Cascades," Scott declares, "Rainier is in a class by itself in terms of risk to human life and property."

"Rainier is covered with thirty-six square miles of perennial snow and ice," muses Carolyn Driedger, a hydrologist with the Cascades Volcano Observatory who has carefully measured the size and thickness of the mountain's glaciers. During the eruption of Mount St. Helens, she says, three-quarters of that volcano's glacial ice melted over a very short time, creating gargantuan mudflows that ran all the way to the Columbia River, filling its channels with enough debris to disrupt international shipping for three months. "And remember that St. Helens," Driedger points out, "only had about four percent as much year-round ice and snow as Rainier has. That's pretty sobering to think about."

Rainier's prodigious mantle of ice contributes to the potential danger in a less obvious, more insidious way as well. The peak's subterranean heat is continuously melting its glaciers from below, feeding water into a complex system of geothermal aquifers. Constantly circulating through the mountain, this abundance of hot liquid combines with sulfur-bearing gases to produce acids that are eroding Rainier from the inside out, undermining its structural integrity. "The entire edifice of the mountain is stewing in its own hot chemical juices," explains Scott, "and as a consequence it's becoming increasingly rotten and unstable."

Geologists, who call this phenomenon hydrothermal alteration, have only recently begun to appreciate its impact on Mount Rainier. "We don't have a very complete picture of what's going on up there yet," says Don Swanson, a geologist with the U.S. Geological Survey and a contributor to the 1994 National Research Council report. "But the hydrothermal alteration of all that rock is alarming to contemplate. I firmly believe that learning the extent of the alteration is among the most important things to find out about Rainier."

Most of what we know thus far comes from the efforts of Tom Sisson and David Zimbelman, geologists who have spent many months on the mountain, painstakingly studying and mapping it. "It's extremely hard work," Zimbelman admits. Because altered rock is inherently unstable, he and Sisson had to climb some of Rainier's more dangerous slopes to conduct their research.

The research has shed considerable light on the degree to which strong acids percolating through Rainier's innards are transforming solid rock into soft, crumbly clay, a process that is readily apparent on the rim of the summit crater. The thin air up here reeks of rotten eggs: the telltale scent of hydrogen sulfide gas, which condenses and mixes with water to form sulfuric acid, the primary agent of alteration on Rainier. Around the steaming summit fumaroles, clumps of reddish-brown mud cling to the spikes of climbers' crampons. This spongy stuff is hydrothermally altered rock.

Zimbelman and Sisson have discovered bands of weak, highly altered rock that locally penetrate the mountain. It is the nature of clay to absorb water, and expand when it does so. As zones of newly altered rock on Rainier swell with moisture, dry out, and re-expand, the clay acts as a sort of natural crowbar, prying apart the more solid rock around it, further weakening the edifice.

As soon as part of Rainier grows sufficiently rickety, a catastrophic lahar is bound to result. "What would it take to trigger a significant mudflow?" asks Zimbelman. "Certainly an earthquake could do the job. But so could a much lesser event like a minor steam explosion. You have all this gravitationally unstable rock becoming weaker and weaker; eventually it's going to reach a point where it won't take much of a jolt to break off a big piece of mountain and send it tumbling toward Puget Sound. In fact, you could have a major sector collapse without any triggering mechanism at all. That's what's so scary: something huge could come down simply under its own weight, with no advance warning."

When Rainier is viewed from southern Puget Sound, it looks like a large part of the summit cone is missing, as though removed by some ice-cream scoop. The cliffs that form the walls of the hollow are mottled with yellowish-orange splotches: zones of rotten, clay-rich altered rock that hold clues to what happened here. The scooped-out area is called the Sunset Amphitheater, and its existence hints at what can happen when a really big piece of the mountain lets go. The hollow is where the Electron Mudflow started.

Around the corner from the Sunset Amphitheater, on the north face of the mountain, scars from an even bigger cataclysm are visible with the naked eye from downtown Seattle. They were left behind by the Osceola Mudflow, the largest known lahar ever spawned by Mount Rainier. It came thundering down about 5,000 years ago, when something—perhaps an earthquake or a buildup of steam within the volcano, perhaps nothing more than the tug of gravity on hydrothermally weakened rock—caused the upper 2,000 feet of the peak to cleave off and slide away. A dusting of airborne ash sprinkled over the region at the time of the mudflow indicates that it was accompanied by a modest volcanic eruption, but many geologists have come to believe that the landslide may have triggered the eruption, rather than vice versa.

The Osceola Mudflow began as an avalanche of mind-boggling size, carrying sixty times as much rubble as the lahar that wiped out Armero in 1985. Much of the flow consisted of clay saturated with geothermal fluids, an avalanche of semi-liquid muck that roared downslope at a speed in excess of 100 miles per hour.

As it reached the base of the mountain and churned down the valleys of the White, Green, and Puyallup Rivers, the lahar slowed to between 30 and 50 miles per hour, but it nevertheless scoured the earth of everything in its path. Thanks to its high clay content, the Osceola Mudflow was what geologists call a cohesive lahar: a thick, gooey mass viscous enough to suspend house-size boulders and 200-foot trees within its flow. Indeed, it swallowed up entire forests and carried them down onto the plains below.

Cohesive lahars tend to travel farther and pack a greater punch than more dilute, clay-poor, noncohesive lahars, and the Osceola Mudflow was no exception. It ran all the way to Puget Sound, whose shores lay considerably east of where they do now. The lahar blanketed at least 200 square miles with a layer of concrete-like muck twenty-five feet deep, burying the sites of present-day Orting, Enumclaw, Auburn, Puyallup, Kent, and Sumner and some of the Tacoma waterfront.

If a similar lahar came down Rainier tomorrow, it would take about one to two hours to reach the densely populated lowlands. According to Kevin Scott, residents of Orting would see "a wall of trees, rocks, and mud rolling down the canyon of the Carbon River at perhaps thirty miles per hour. The sound would be deafening and the earth would tremble. In Armero, survivors reported hearing a loud roar and feeling the ground shake when the lahar was still five kilometers away, but they didn't know what was happening—they thought it was an earthquake—so they didn't run to high ground."

Hoping to avoid such deadly confusion, in February of last year the Orting Fire Department hand-delivered copies of an emergency evacuation plan to each of the town's roughly 3,000 residents. The plan explains that if a debris flow is expected, sirens will sound throughout Orting, indicating that people should immediately leave town via evacuation routes described on an attached map. In conjunction with the plan, the local schools regularly practice lahar evacuation drills.

"The last time the schools held a drill," says Orting fire chief Scott Fielding, "all the kids were out of the city and bused to high ground in fifteen minutes. I'm more concerned about our adult citizens. We've told them, 'When you hear the sirens, get in your car and leave! Immediately!' But adults are more likely to doubt the seriousness of the situation, to question it, to fool around. Realistically, I doubt we'd get more than 50 or 60 percent of the people to actually evacuate."

Fielding acknowledges that for the evacuation plan to work at all, moreover, the town will have to have some advance warning that the mud is bearing down. "And at present," he laments, "no early-detection system is in place. If someone up toward the mountain doesn't happen to see the debris flow and phone the fire department, it's going to be bad news for the people downstream. Personally, I live on a hill above town, so I sleep well at night. But I worry about my friends who live on the valley floor."

Scientists and government officials have discussed establishing a network of electronic sensing devices in each of the threatened drainages to sound a warning when a lahar is on the way. Such a system, however, would probably be far from foolproof. "The technology for implementing something like that would be pretty straightforward," says Steve Malone. "The problem will be maintaining it in the long term, and getting people to take it seriously when the alarm goes off after decades or even centuries without anything happening."

What, then, can we who live in the shadow of the mountain do to protect our lives and property the next time a tsunami of mud comes rumbling down from the heights? Civil engineers have suggested constructing massive containment dams in each of the half-dozen river drainages that snake down from Rainier to Puget Sound. Such structures could be designed to catch most of the sediment released by a lahar.

Although containment dams would probably stop a lahar, says Patrick Pringle, a geologist with the Washington State Department of Natural Resources, "the cost of building and maintaining them would be substantial, and I don't think the public is willing to commit those kinds of funds in this economic climate. It's hard to galvanize people to do anything until after a disaster has already happened. Mudflows occur so infrequently that people would rather just take their chances. They'd rather spend their tax money on a new baseball stadium. Such dams would also pose environmental problems."

In the absence of containment dams and a reliable early-warning program, an obvious way to reduce the risk would be to enact zoning laws that would prevent people from building homes or businesses in the path of documented mudflows. "But most of the land we're talking about is prime real estate," laments Don Swanson. "It's probably unrealistic to think that very much of it will be placed off-limits."

Given fiscal and political realities, Swanson, Scott, Pringle, and other experts believe the best course of action for the time being is to learn as much as possible about the hazards posed by the mountain and aggressively share that knowledge with the public. Toward that end, the International Association of Volcanology and Chemistry of the Earth's Interior has designated Rainier, along with fourteen other mountains worldwide, a "Decade Volcano: an unusually dangerous volcano earmarked for intensive study."

"We're trying to come up with hard statistical data," says Pringle, "actual numbers people can use to get a handle on the risk. We want to give people enough knowledge to make rational decisions concerning their options. The challenge is to get the public's attention without alarming anybody unnecessarily."

"It's extremely hard to quantify these kinds of risks," Swanson concedes. "How do you put large but infrequent hazards into any sort of meaningful statistical context? A catastrophic mudflow is not likely to happen on Rainier in our lifetime. But it will happen somewhere down the road, in one or more generations. And when it does, a lot of people will lose everything."

DEATH AND ANGER ON EVEREST

For many years, the most lucrative commercial guiding opera-
tion on Mount Everest has been a company called Himalayan Experience, or Himex, which is owned by a New Zealand
mountaineer named Russell Brice. In the spring of 2012, more
than a month into the climbing season, he became increasingly worried about a bulge of glacial ice three hundred yards
wide that was frozen tenuously to the side of Everest's West
Shoulder, hanging like a massive sword of Damocles directly
over the main route up the Nepal side of Everest. Brice's clients
(called "members" in the parlance of Himalayan mountaineering), Western guides, and sherpas repeatedly had to climb
beneath the threatening ice bulge as they moved up and down
the mountain to acclimatize and establish a series of higher
camps necessary for their summit assault. One day Brice
timed how long it took his head guide, Adrian Ballinger ("who
is incredibly fast," he wrote in the blog post excerpted below)
to climb through the most hazardous terrain:

> [I]t took him 22 min[utes] from the beginning to the end of
> the danger zone. For the Sherpas carrying a heavy load it
> took 30 min[utes] and most of our members took between
> 45 min[utes] and one hour to walk underneath this danger-
> ous cliff. In my opinion, this is far too long to be exposed to
> such a danger and when I see around 50 people moving
> underneath the cliff at one time, it scares me.

Adding to Brice's concern, some of his most experienced sherpas, ordinarily exceedingly stoical men, approached him to say the conditions on the mountain made them fear for their lives. One of them actually broke down in tears as he confessed this. So on May 7, 2012, Brice made an announcement that shocked most of the thousand people camped at the base of Everest: he was pulling all his guides, members, and sherpas off the mountain, packing up their tents and equipment, and heading home. He was widely criticized for this decision in 2012, and not just by clients who were forced to abandon their dreams of climbing the world's highest mountain without receiving a refund for the 43,000 euros they had paid him in advance. Many of the other expedition leaders also thought Brice was wildly overreacting. The reputation of Himex took a major hit.

After what happened last Friday, though, it's hard to argue with Brice's call. On April 18, shortly before 7:00 A.M. local time, an overhanging wedge of ice the size of a Beverly Hills mansion broke loose from the same ice bulge that had frightened Brice into leaving Everest in 2012. As it crashed onto the slope below, the ice shattered into truck-size chunks and hurtled toward some fifty climbers laboring slowly upward through the Khumbu Icefall, a jumbled maze of unstable ice towers that looms above the 17,600-foot base camp. The climbers in the line of fire were at approximately 19,000 feet when the avalanche struck. Of the twenty-five men hit by the falling ice, sixteen were killed, all of them Nepalis working for guided climbing teams. Three of the bodies were buried beneath the frozen debris and may never be found.

Although many news reports indicated that all the victims were Sherpas, the legendary mountain people who comprise just half of one percent of the Nepali population, three of the sixteen were members of other, much larger ethnic groups: one was Gurung, one was Tamang, and one was a member of the Hindu Chhetri caste. All, however, were employed as high-altitude climbing sherpas, with a lowercase *s*—an elite profession that deservedly commands respect and admiration from mountaineers around the world.

It was the worst climbing accident in the history of Everest, twice as deadly as the infamous storm in May 1996 that killed eight people, the subject of my book, *Into Thin Air* (four of my teammates accounted for half of that grim tally). But dying on Everest has been an occupational hazard for sherpas ever since a team led by George Leigh Mallory to attempt the Tibetan side of the peak in 1922 became the first mountaineers to ascend higher than the lower flanks of the mountain. In the final days of that expedition, seven sherpas from Darjeeling, India, were swept to their deaths in an avalanche. Sad to say, the job hasn't gotten any safer for sherpas with the passage of time. According to a piece by Jonah Ogles posted on out sideonline.com, the death rate for climbing sherpas on Everest from 2004 until now was twelve times higher than the death rate for U.S. military personnel deployed in Iraq from 2003 to 2007.

There is no denying that climbing Everest is a preposterously dangerous undertaking for the members who provide the sherpas' income. But running counter to the disturbing trend among sherpas, climbing Everest has actually grown significantly safer for Western guides and members in recent years, according to the available data. This can be attributed to a number of factors: Western climbers now use bottled oxygen much more liberally than they did in the past; weather forecasts are much more accurate than they were eighteen or twenty years ago; and many Western climbers now prophylactically dose themselves with dexamethasone, a powerful steroid, when they ascend above 22,000 feet, which has proven to be an effective strategy for minimizing the risk of contracting high-altitude cerebral edema (HACE) and high-altitude pulmonary edema (HAPE), potentially fatal ailments that are common on Everest.

During the seventy-six years from the first attempt on Everest in 1921 through 1996, when I was guided up Everest, 144 people died and the summit was reached 630 times, a ratio of one death for every four successful ascents. Notably, over the eighteen years that have passed since 1996, 104 people have died and the summit has been reached 6,241 times—one death for every 60 ascents. Furthermore, non-sherpas accounted for only 71 of these deaths, which equates to just one death for every 88 ascents.

The reason the risk remains so much greater for sherpas can be traced to several factors. Sherpas aren't provided with nearly as much bottled oxygen, because it is so expensive to purchase and to stock on the upper mountain, and they tend to be much better acclimatized than Westerners. Sherpas are almost never given dexamethasone prophylactically, because they don't have personal physicians in their villages who will prescribe the drug on request. And perhaps most significant, sherpas do all the heavy lifting on Everest, literally and figuratively. The mostly foreign-owned guiding companies assign the most dangerous and physically demanding jobs to their sherpa staff, thereby mitigating the risk to their Western guides and members, whose backpacks seldom hold much more than a water bottle, a camera, an extra jacket, and lunch. The work sherpas are paid to do—carrying loads, installing aluminum ladders in the Khumbu Icefall, stringing and anchoring thousands of feet of rope—requires them to spend vastly more time on the most dangerous parts of the mountain, particularly in the Icefall—the shattered, creaking, ever-shifting expanse of glacier that extends from just above base camp at 17,600 feet to the 19,500-foot elevation. The fact that members and Western guides now suck down a lot more bottled oxygen is wonderful for them, but it means the sherpas have to carry those additional oxygen bottles through the Icefall for the Westerners to use.

Historically, more Everest climbers have perished from severe weather, HACE, HAPE, exhaustion, falling from steep terrain, or some combination of these hazards than being crushed or buried in the Khumbu Icefall. This seems to be changing, however. Accurate weather forecasting has reduced the risk of being surprised by a killer storm like the one that struck in 1996. But the pronounced warming of the Himalayan climate in recent years has made the Icefall more unstable than ever, and there is still no way to predict when a serac is going to topple over. And sherpas spend much, much more time in the Icefall than their Western employers.

In 1996, for example, I made four round trips through the Khumbu Icefall: three circuits as I progressively acclimatized to 24,000 feet during the month of April, and then one final round trip on my journey to the 29,035-foot summit and back. I was terrified each of the eight times I moved through the frozen chaos, which usually took more than three hours to ascend even with my nearly empty backpack, and slightly less than an hour to descend. In contrast, each of the sherpas supporting my team's ascent was required to make something like thirty trips through the Icefall, often while carrying 80-pound loads of food, propane, and bottled oxygen.

These days, moreover, members are apt to spend even less time in the Icefall than I did when I was on Everest eighteen years ago. It's becoming increasingly common for Western guides and members to acclimatize in hypobaric chambers before they arrive in Nepal, and/or on other, less hazardous Himalayan peaks in advance of their summit assaults, greatly reducing the number of times they must expose themselves to the perils of the Icefall. Some members now make only a single round trip through it, while each of the sherpas supporting them must still pass through that hazardous terrain between two and three dozen times. Most Western climbers feel more than a little guilty about this, but none that I know of have ever offered to take an extra lap through the Icefall with a heavy load in order to reduce a sherpa's exposure.

The statistics suggesting Everest has become safe for members may in fact be giving Westerners a false sense of security, however. The astounding number of climbers who now attempt to reach the summit on the limited number of days when the weather is favorable presents a new kind of hazard. A notorious photo shot by Ralf Dujmovits in May 2012 showed more than 150 people attached to a series of fixed ropes as they ascended the Lhotse Face toward the South Col of Everest, jammed together so tightly they had to move in lockstep. The static weight of all these people and their gear was well over 30,000 pounds. If some mishap had occurred that caused more than a handful of the climbers to put their full weight on one of these ropes simultaneously, the shock to the anchors securing the ropes to the ice could easily have caused them to fail, resulting in the climbers falling, en masse, 2,000 or more feet to the base of the Lhotse Face. If such an accident should come to pass in the future (which isn't far-fetched), the death count for both members and sherpas would be horrific.

In any event, no Western members or guides were killed or injured in last week's avalanche. At the moment, in the immediate aftermath, almost everyone climbing on the Nepal side of Everest has retreated to base camp to try to come to grips with the catastrophe. Most of them, sherpas and foreign climbers alike, are reeling from the unprecedented loss of life. At least one expedition has already announced it will be abandoning the mountain. For the foreign climbers, to go home now will mean forfeiting most or all of the $50,000 to $90,000 they have spent to be guided up Everest. For the sherpas who make the guided ascents possible, however, to quit now after only a few weeks' wages will be an even greater economic sacrifice, relatively speaking.

Depending on their talent, experience, foreign-language skills, how many loads they carry up and down the mountain, and how generously they're tipped by their clients, climbing sherpas will generally take home between $2,000 and $8,000 at the conclusion of an Everest expedition, which commences for them in late March and typically ends around the first of June. If a climbing sherpa dies on the job, his family will receive a million rupees (approximately $10,500) from the insurance his employer is required to provide. By any reasonable measure, neither these wages nor insurance payouts are fair compensation for the risk involved. But in Nepal, where the median annual income is less than $600, most of the sherpas' countrymen would eagerly take similar risks for the opportunity to receive that kind of pay.

Nevertheless, on April 20, after holding several emotional, contentious meetings at Everest basecamp, the climbing sherpas announced they would go on strike unless the Nepali government agreed to meet thirteen demands within a week. The threat of a work stoppage was provoked by the sherpas' outrage over the Nepali government's offer to provide just 40,000 rupees—slightly more than $400—to the families of the sherpas killed in the avalanche to defray their funeral expenses. Among the sherpas' demands are that the government increase this compensation to approximately $1,000 per family; provide $10,000 to climbing sherpas who have been seriously disabled; establish a permanent relief fund for injured sherpas with a portion of the $10,000 permit fees every Western Everest climber is charged by the Nepali government; double the current insurance benefit provided by the guiding companies to $21,000; require the guiding companies to pay sherpas their salaries even if they call off the remainder of the

2014 Everest climbing season; and establish a monument in Kathmandu to memorialize the deceased sherpas.

The collective anger and resentment expressed by the sherpas over the past few days is unprecedented. On April 20, Tim and Becky Rippel, the owners of guiding company called Peak Freaks that lost a sherpa named Mingma Tenzing to a fatal case of HAPE earlier in the month, stated in a blog post:

> As we suggested in a previous post the Sherpa guides are heating up, emotions are running wild and demands are being made to share the wealth with the Sherpa people on the table. Now that there are more Sherpa operators today on Everest, they've come to learn how much the government of Nepal makes in revenues from Everest expeditions and they are asking for a share. This is their time and under very unfortunate circumstances.... In any case things are getting very complicated and there is a lot of tension here and it's growing.... Peak Freaks is in support of the Sherpa people any which way it goes. They are our family, our brothers and sisters and the muscle on Everest. We follow their lead, we are guests here.

DESCENT TO MARS

I awoke facedown in the dirt, drenched with sweat, engulfed in darkness so absolute that it made no difference whether my eyes were open or closed. Groggy and disoriented, I sat bolt upright and tried to figure out where I was. Then I remembered, and had to fight back a wave of panic: I was a thousand feet underground, in the far reaches of a claustrophobic labyrinth called Lechuguilla Cave.

I groped inside my sleeping bag until I found a flashlight, and flicked it on. The beam illuminated a low, domed space the size of a parking garage festooned with preposterous limestone udders. Nine other people were sprawled on the ground nearby. Three of them—Chris McKay, Penny Boston, and Larry Lemke—were NASA scientists who had descended into this disquieting netherworld because, as McKay had explained earlier with an apparent non sequitur, "We want to know if there's life on Mars."

It was not easy getting here. The mission had been launched two days earlier, from a scorched New Mexico hillside freckled with prickly pear and lechuguilla plants—the spiny agave after which the cave was named. Located in Carlsbad Caverns National Park, just a few miles from Carlsbad Caverns, the unmarked entrance to Lechuguilla is a forbidding vertical shaft. Wearing helmets, headlamps, mountaineering harnesses, and fifty-pound backpacks, we attached ourselves to a frayed rope, shuffled backward over the edge, and rappelled

one by one into the gloom. Within moments, we found ourselves in an environment that felt more alien than any place I'd
ever been.

Presently considered to be one of the most spectacular and
geologically unique caves in the world, until nine years ago
Lechuguilla was known to extend no further than its 90-foot
entrance pit. At one edge of the pit, however, recreational cavers noticed a distinct breeze blowing from a pile of jumbled
rocks, inspiring them to probe deeper. On May 25, 1986, after
a decade of intermittent excavation, three men dug through
the last of the rubble and discovered a narrow, twisting pas-
sageway leading down into the bowels of the earth.

One of the trio who made this discovery was a celebrated
caver named Rick Bridges, and it was he who led the NASA
team into Lechuguilla last December. The trip down was long
and arduous. The temperature remained a constant 67 degrees
Fahrenheit, which initially seemed quite comfortable. The
humidity hovered near 100 percent, however, so the slightest
physical effort produced a flood of perspiration that soaked
our clothing and never dried.

Bearing all our food and equipment on our backs, we
scrambled through a chaos of truck-size boulders, slithered
like lizards down narrow slots, and dangled above chasms
that appeared bottomless. At times, we used ropes and technical caving gear to rappel into pits that overhung on all sides.
I knew that the only way to return to the surface five days
hence would be to climb strands of rope we left behind as
we descended, so my anxiety grew as we pressed deeper and
deeper underground.

Our battery-powered headlamps became our most valuable possessions. Indeed, each of us carried at least two backup
lights, because without a means of illumination we would be
blind, helpless, and stranded. More than eighty miles of pas-
sageway have been discovered thus far in Lechuguilla, a natural

maze of mind-boggling complexity that looks like a tangle of spaghetti when plotted on a three-dimensional map. Bridges guided us down a route that corkscrewed through a devious geologic honeycomb.

Although fraught with hazards, Lechuguilla is a place of phantasmal beauty. Cramped, twisting passages opened suddenly into spaces as voluminous as Madison Square Garden, the walls of which sparkled with brilliant white crystals. Opalescent "cave pearls" lay in clusters at the bottom of shallow pools. Fragile balloons of hydromagnesite, formed by expanding gases, decorated the ceiling of a low tunnel. In several places, delicate gypsum "chandeliers" hung from the roof like flocked Christmas trees. Everywhere I turned, there was one or another exotic embellishment, otherworldly and dazzling.

The NASA crew, however, was uninterested in such comely sights. What had lured them into Lechuguilla, rather, were the ugliest parts of the cave: a handful of comparatively unadorned areas coated with a nasty, mud-like substance known as corrosion residue. Cavers called it "gorilla shit," and it was impossible to touch the stuff without becoming filthy, but McKay, Boston, and Lemke found it extremely stimulating. They believed that corrosion residue might hold important clues about Mars—an object of passionate interest to all three scientists, and their sole reason for visiting Lechuguilla. Specifically, they theorized that corrosion residue might answer crucial questions about whether life exists on the red planet.

"You cavers," McKay explained to Bridges, "have a pathological defect that allows you to think it's fun to spend five days underground, getting dirty, lugging fifty-pound packs up and down cliffs. You have my sympathy, and I hope someday they find a cure for your disease, but for Penny and Larry and me this is not fun. I'd much rather be home right now. But the corrosion residue is so exciting—and what it might tell us about Mars is so exciting—that we're willing to come down into this cave to suffer miserably and grunt like pigs in order to study it."

Photographs of Mars show that water once flowed there, and long ago, it may also have had a fairly substantial atmosphere. Today the planet is a harsh place, however, brutally cold and without liquid water. The atmosphere is exceedingly thin. "The surface would seem to be very inhospitable to life of any kind," McKay acknowledges. "If life does exist on Mars, you'd expect to find it underground. Organisms would be shielded from the intense ultraviolet radiation there. A volcanic heat source might conceivably generate liquid water from subsurface ice. In the absence of sunlight and organic matter, any extant life would have to derive its energy entirely from mineral sources." To put it simply, such life would have to eat rocks.

Creatures of that ilk do in fact exist here on earth. Biologists call them autotrophic organisms, and they have been found living around hot volcanic vents on the ocean floor, among other places. Not a lot is known about them, but McKay, Boston, and Lemke speculate that similar forms of life might flourish in caves on Mars—and in the dark recesses of Lechuguilla Cave.

Deep in Lechuguilla, many of the fundamental reference points that lend order to everyday existence are absent. There is no weather in the cave, no natural horizon, no noise, no sunrise or sunset, no way to tell what time it is, what day, what year. Lacking visual cues, we find ourselves keeping odd hours. Crawling out of his bivouac sack at ten A.M., Larry Lemke—a compact, forty-seven-year-old engineer from NASA's Ames Research Center—declares, "My biological clock is already drifting. I seem to fall into a twenty-five-hour day down here—just like you would on Mars, which has twenty-four-and-a-half-hour days."

Stiff and hungover from the strenuous trip down, the team assembles for breakfast on a gravelly hummock. This chamber, named Deep Secrets by the cavers who discovered it, will serve as our base camp for four nights. I dig into a plastic pouch of cold freeze-dried chili left over from yesterday's dinner—not because it tastes good, but because if I don't eat it, I'll have to carry it back up to the surface. To keep Lechuguilla pristine, everything that came in with us must go out with us. Even human waste is sealed carefully in Ziploc bags and carried out.

We are on our own down here, cut off from the rest of the world. The implications of that are not lost on anyone. In 1991, an experienced caver named Emily Mobley broke her tibia not far from the Deep Secrets camp when an immense rock rolled onto her leg. It took the combined efforts of 180 cavers four days to evacuate her.

Our isolation—and our need to be self-sufficient—is analogous to a space journey, suggests Lemke, who has designed several hypothetical missions to Mars for NASA. "This cave is an alien world," he says, "with its own special rules and hazards. Living down here is difficult. It's given me some practical insights into the challenge of doing research halfway across the solar system."

The research scheduled for this morning's agenda will be conducted a mere quarter mile from camp, but getting to the site is problematic enough to keep plenty of insights flowing Lemke's way. After loading up our backpacks with scientific paraphernalia, we negotiate a passage called the Fortress of Chaos, which is rather like squirming through an enormous chunk of Swiss cheese. At the top of the Fortress, a strand of rope hangs from a hole overhead. Clipping small, ratchet-like devices to the rope (called ascenders, they slide upward freely, but grip the line when weighted), we haul ourselves toward the ceiling with much huffing and puffing.

The rope leads through a sugary white flue of gypsum crystals to emerge in a chamber stacked with huge, tottering boulders. When they see that the entire room is coated with a filthy brown scum of corrosion residue, McKay, Boston, and Lemke grow ecstatic.

Chris McKay, forty, is a 6-foot-6-inch beanpole of a man with a scraggly beard and a wry sense of humor. Forty-one-year-old Penny Boston is smallish and voluble. A tangle of blond curls cascades haphazardly from beneath her helmet. Neither McKay nor Boston is particularly athletic, or could be called a thrill seeker. Each left behind a spouse and a young child to make the trip into Lechuguilla.

Given that both McKay and Boston claim to abhor being underground, one has to wonder why they didn't simply ask a team of experienced cavers to collect a sample of corrosion residue and deliver it to their labs, thereby obviating the need for either scientist to suffer the claustrophobic hardships of Lechuguilla.

Such a question, McKay observes, "gets to the very nature of fieldwork. Why couldn't we simply use surrogates? I don't really know the answer, but I know it doesn't work. There is just no substitute for being there in person. Experiencing the environment with your own eyes and your full attention—both conscious and unconscious—is essential. Surrogates can't give us the understanding we develop by going into the field ourselves, taking samples in real time, and discussing things on site."

Hence the numerous extended visits McKay has made over the past fifteen years to places such as Mongolia's Gobi Desert, Chile, Siberia, the Canadian Arctic, and the dry valleys of Antarctica—all of which are extremely remote and inhospitable, yet have provided McKay and his NASA colleagues with invaluable theoretical musings about the nature of life on the red planet.

"As you might imagine," McKay continues, "the same question comes up time and time again during discussions about whether it's necessary to send humans to Mars. I happen to think that it is necessary, since we won't know exactly what we're looking for until we get there. We'll be depending a lot on the intuition of the scientists involved. They'll know what's important when they see it."

McKay and Boston met as accelerated students at Florida Atlantic University in 1972 and have remained fast friends over the ensuing decades. Both have been fascinated with space since childhood. In 1976, when the Viking missions landed on Mars, that fascination crystallized into an infatuation with the fourth planet. "I remember the Viking landings as incredibly thrilling events," Boston says.

"Viking told us very clearly that all the elements for life were present on Mars," says McKay, "yet there was no life there—the lights were on, but nobody was home. That really piqued our interest. Was there life on Mars in the past? Could it harbor life in the future?"

McKay and Boston were both graduate students at the University of Colorado when Viking landed. In 1981, as a school project with a half-dozen other Mars fanatics, they put together an ambitious seminar christened the "Case for Mars" conference, the primary goal of which was to advance an argument for the human exploration of the red planet.

"We were just a bunch of students," Boston concedes. "We had no money, no influence. Basically, we started calling up famous Mars scientists and inviting them to our conference, and much to everyone's surprise some big names like Conway Snyder and Ben Clark agreed to come." It proved to be a roaring success, and was reconvened every three years thereafter. A passionate, if unofficial, network of Mars scientists and aerospace engineers coalesced around these parleys; dedicated to keeping Mars exploration on the national agenda, the group started calling itself the Mars Underground.

McKay is quick to point out that the Underground is not interested in putting a person on Mars merely as a grand adventure or symbolic act. They believe quite strongly that it should be more than an Apollo-like exercise in national chest thumping. "We don't want to simply go to Mars, say 'Hi!' and come home," he insists. "We hope to conduct serious research there. We want to know if there is life on Mars or has been in the past. Imagine what it would mean to discover that we are not alone in the solar system? Such knowledge would have a profound impact on our understanding of life."

Facing a head-high limestone boulder plastered top to bottom with gorilla shit, Penny Boston places four laboratory slides on a narrow ledge. On a subsequent trip, she will collect them to see if any bacterial cultures have taken hold. Nearby, Chris McKay extracts a speck of fluffy brownish-orange corrosion residue with a Swiss Army knife and places it on a handheld electronic pH meter. The gauge registers 1.3, prompting him to exclaim, "Wow, this stuff is *acid*. No wonder it's eating up the limestone."

Corrosion residue is typically found in relatively lofty reaches of the cave, where updrafts of warm air collide with cooler rock. According to the conventional wisdom, the stuff is the by-product by an inorganic chemical reaction between humid, acidic air and the soluble limestone. The Mars Underground crew has an entirely different theory, believing corrosion residue to be biologic in origin. "It's our hypothesis," says Penny Boston, gesturing to the brown crud covering the rocks around her, "that all this nasty stuff has been produced by bugs—a population of microbes native to this cave."

When Lechuguilla was first explored in the late 1980s, it was assumed to be virtually sterile. The rubble that had hidden the entrance from spelunkers had effectively sealed off the cave from the outside world. Even the water in the cave was free from surface contamination: analysis showed no trace of tritium, which meant that all the water now in Lechuguilla percolated into the cave before the widespread nuclear testing of the 1940s and 1950s.

As cavers ventured into the depths of the cavern, they came across the bones of a few stray bats, and even the fossilized remains of a prehistoric camelid (indicating that long ago Lechuguilla was accessible from the surface), but the deeper reaches of the labyrinth appeared to be completely devoid of life.

Then in 1990, a government geologist named Kim Cunningham made an astonishing discovery. While using a scanning electron microscope to study the mineral composition of a chunk of calcite collected in Lechuguilla, he noticed some peculiar, filamentous strands. "Kim's not a biologist," says Boston, "but he's a bright boy. He thought these things looked an awful lot like some kind of fossilized microbial life."

Shortly thereafter, Larry Lemke's wife was watching a National Geographic television special about Lechuguilla. "Larry," she called to him in the next room, "you should come in here and take a look at this." Lemke arrived in time to see a brief mention of Cunningham's discovery. "A lightbulb immediately went off in my head," he says. There ensued a marathon cross-country conference call between Lemke, Cunningham, McKay, and Boston. The upshot was a NASA mission to search for microbial life in Lechuguilla.

Microbes may be tiny, but they have to eat—they need to draw on some source of external energy. "In most caves," explains McKay, "the microbes you find eat organic stuff—bat guano, say, or other nutrients washed down from the outside.

What's so interesting about Lechuguilla is that it's isolated from the surface, so there is no sunlight for photosynthesis, and no source of organic energy. Any bugs living down here have to be metabolizing inorganic minerals."

The majority of the world's limestone caves were dissolved from the surrounding bedrock by mild carbonic acid. Lechuguilla is fairly unique in that it was probably formed by sulfuric acid that percolated up from nearby petroleum fields as hydrogen sulfide gas. The copious deposits of gypsum in Lechuguilla were created as the sulfuric acid dissolved the limestone. Sulfur, also plentiful in the cave, was another by-product.

McKay and his colleagues speculate that this abundance of sulfur serves as an important energy source for a complex microbial ecosystem, the most visible sign of which is the wealth of corrosion residue. The NASA folks believe that corrosion residue is organic waste produced by rock-eating autotrophic bacteria. It's not gorilla poop that coats these cave walls, in other words—it's germ poop.

McKay and Boston are now working to prove this hypothesis, building on earlier research by Kim Cunningham and biologists Larry Mallory and Diana Northrup. On this and future trips into Lechuguilla, they will collect cultures of microbes from around the cave, identify them in the laboratory, and try to determine their relationship to one another. The results should ultimately help them with the question they're really interested in: "Do bugs like this," as Boston puts it, "also live on Mars?"

She and her colleagues admit that they are still a long way from proving that the corrosion residue in Lechuguilla is produced by microorganisms, let alone demonstrating that similar critters live on Mars. Back at the Deep Secrets base camp, squatting in the dirt over a dinner of reconstituted chicken Tetrazzini, Lemke emphasizes that "landing humans on Mars to prove that microbial life exists there, or once existed there, is a very daunting challenge. The round trip would take a minimum of six hundred to a thousand days. The technological obstacles would be huge."

Even if the United States made putting a person on Mars a national priority and slated it for the fast track, says Boston, "it would take at least fifteen years for it to happen. And right now Mars isn't a priority. We're doing this research on a shoestring."

"I think we're at a crisis point," warns Lemke. "For a long time the space program was a way to conduct the Cold War by other means. We all got behind the Apollo program to beat the Russians to the moon, and as a cultural event, it made the entire country feel great. Now that we've won the race, we have to ask ourselves if we're willing as a nation to continue doing space exploration for its own merit. I think it's an open question."

Surprisingly, given their abiding passion for the red planet, Lemke, Boston, and McKay are in agreement that it would be a mistake to launch a crash program to put a person on Mars. "There are too many downsides," explains Boston. "We don't want to go through Apollo again—the goal becomes simply getting there. We want to achieve something more meaningful. We think it's better to proceed slowly and thoughtfully."

A go-slow approach is fine, says Lemke, "as long as you can sustain a public commitment to the program's goals over the long haul. That's very difficult in the face of so many competing demands for funding."

"Which brings us back to what we're doing in this cave," McKay chimes in. "Part of our work is to establish a clear goal: to answer the question 'Why go to Mars?' We think the best answer is 'To look for life.' People can grasp that. It has universal appeal. By going to places like Lechuguilla—by digging up weird life-forms and saying, 'Look, folks, this is interesting stuff, and it could also be happening on another planet'—we hope to build enthusiasm for eventually going to Mars."

Nobody in the Underground thinks getting to Mars will be easy (politically or otherwise), but they are patient people, and determined. The trip into Lechuguilla has only fanned the flames of their ardor. In 1998, NASA plans to land another unmanned spacecraft on Mars, and the folks in the Mars Underground are aggressively pushing to equip that lander with drilling equipment, enabling it to make at least a cursory probe of the planet's subsurface environment.

Assessing the prospects for the Underground's research efforts, Boston says, "All in all, we're pretty ecstatic and fired up." Nevertheless, she adds, "I think there's a major object lesson in this for those of us planning the search for past or present life on Mars. It's damn hard even here on earth, where we are awash in colleagues to consult and sophisticated laboratories to work in. We've only just begun to convince other scientists that there is indeed life in Lechuguilla. How then to convince them that there is life on Mars when we someday arrive there?"

Out in front of the NASA team, hours into the long ascent from the depths of Lechuguilla, I round a bend to encounter something so strange and unexpected that it takes me a few moments to recognize what it is: a cool breeze blowing across my grimy, sweat-drenched skin. A little farther and I arrive at something even stranger: a ray of sunlight, leaking exquisitely through a crooked fissure overhead. I am almost back to the surface.

The last remaining obstacle is an overhanging, 60-foot climb out of the guano-spackled entrance pit. Muscling up the final strand of free-hanging rope is exhausting, but I am so relieved to be escaping the underworld that I scarcely notice my labored breathing and cramping arms. Just before noon, I pull over the lip and emerge into a brilliant New Mexico morning.

Sunlight washes over my chest and face. I inhale a greedy lungful of desert air, savoring the scent of juniper and sage. The colors that flood my light-starved retinas—the blue of the sky, a pale green drift of cactus, the creamy palette of the clouds—seem electric, surreal, almost overwhelming. An involuntary whoop of joy erupts from my throat. I feel as if I've just escaped from a supermax prison.

Inebriated with a newfound appreciation of the ordinary, I imagine for a moment that I'm getting a taste of what an astronaut might experience on his or her return from a mission to Mars. Then I remember that I've been underground, away from the world, for a mere five days. My God, I wonder: If I'm this discombobulated by an absence of less than a week, what would it feel like to return to earth after a journey of two or three years?

AFTER THE FALL

August 22, 1986, dawned clear and still over Jackson Hole, promising fine weather for climbing in the Tetons. Jim Bridwell rolled groggily out of bed and put on a pot of coffee. Bridwell—the fabled Admiral of Yosemite, the first man to climb El Capitan in a single day, the first to ascend the notorious East Face of the Mooses Tooth in Alaska, a veteran of the planet's most frightening rock walls—was spending a relatively mundane summer working for the Exum Mountain Guide Service and School of American Mountaineering, instructing tourists in the rudiments of rock-climbing. At 8:30 A.M., he called the Exum office and learned that a group of clients who were booked to depart with him that morning on a two-day guided ascent of the Grand Teton had canceled. It was unwelcome news, for Bridwell—perennially strapped for cash and hounded by creditors—could ill afford the loss of income.

A minute later, however, the phone rang, and Bridwell's luck appeared to take a turn for the better: A guide was needed right away to teach an intermediate rock-climbing class; was he interested? "Sure," Bridwell replied without hesitation. He gulped his coffee, grabbed his climbing gear, and hurried off to the Exum headquarters—a small cabin beside Jenny Lake.

The class consisted of four men, all friends, the oldest of whom was an affable, heavyset, forty-one-year-old attorney from Houston named Edward Carrington who had played tight end for the Houston Oilers of the American Football

League from 1967 to 1969. Bridwell made sure that each student had signed a standard acknowledgment of risk form and was outfitted with a helmet and climbing harness; then they all caught a boat to the west shore of Jenny Lake, bound for some crags near Hidden Falls known as the Exum Practice Rocks. The four clients—perhaps slightly awed to find themselves under the tutelage of one of American mountaineering's most notorious and celebrated figures—bantered cheerfully about the climbing to come.

Nobody had any reason to suspect that before the day was over, Edward Carrington would be dead from a bizarre accident, the precise cause of which remains murky to this day. Each year, according to the American Alpine Club, some twenty-five to forty people are killed in climbing accidents in the United States (a fatality rate, according to actuarial experts, that makes climbing slightly less hazardous than operating a power mower), and for the most part these tragedies have little impact beyond the self-contained miasma of grief that descends upon the family and friends of the deceased. Carrington's death, however, would figure prominently in the decision of Yvon Chouinard, founder of this country's oldest and largest manufacturer of climbing hardware, to take down his shingle and quit the business. It would also send legal and financial shock waves through the American mountaineering community for years to come.

According to National Park Service documents, Jim Bridwell's class started off like any other. (Bridwell was unavailable to comment for this article.) The group spent a successful morning at the practice rocks, reviewing the fundamentals of tying in, belaying, and placing hardware for protection, and completed two short climbs along the way. After lunch, they roped together and, with Bridwell in the lead, embarked upon what was meant to be the culmination of Exum's intermediate climbing course: a three-pitch route called the Hole in the

Wall, with a difficulty rating of 5.7. The first two pitches went smoothly enough, and by two P.M., all five men were crowded on a belay ledge in the eponymous Hole, an alcove cut deep into the cliff's granite facade, which to a neophyte climber contemplating the crux moves above can feel both claustrophobic and exposed. Carrington, in fact, mentioned as much to his guide, confiding that the place scared him.

Bridwell reassured his client, made sure everyone was anchored securely, and then edged out of the Hole and worked his way up the final steep slab that led to the top of the route. Carrington was next on the rope. After cautioning his three buddies, "Check your gear!" he started climbing, protected by a snug rope from above. Moving awkwardly off the ledge on the small handholds, Carrington managed to struggle only a short distance away from the Hole before his companions heard him shout, "Hold me!" and watched as he abruptly popped off the rock. Bridwell, alert to the possibility of such a slip, immediately cinched down the rope, arresting Carrington's fall after he'd dropped only a foot or two.

Carrington retreated back to the security of the Hole, composed himself, then gave it another try. Once again, he scrabbled clumsily away from the ledge, and once again, his arms gave out just a few feet from the Hole. Forty feet above, Bridwell heard him cry, "Falling!"

"I felt a short jerk," the guide later told a Park Service investigator, "and then nothing, as if Ed were back on the rock but somehow different. I looked down and saw him falling." In horror and confusion, Bridwell watched him bounce down the rock face, somehow disconnected from the rope. For a moment after starting to fall, Carrington maintained an upright posture, and it was possible to pretend that nothing was really amiss, that something would arrest his slide, that everything would still turn out all right. But then he was flipped upside down by a sharp blow against the cliff and began to tumble like a rag doll, accelerating earthward amid a shower of stones knocked loose by his repeated collisions with the wall. It became apparent not only that Carrington was going to go all the way to the ground, but that he was hurtling directly toward an unsuspecting group of Exum students gathered around their instructor, Peter Lev, at the foot of the climb.

Overcoming his shock, Bridwell managed to blurt out a warning to those below. Lev—part owner of the Exum school—shouted at his four students to scatter. "It was horrible," Lev recalls, still haunted by the memory. "Carrington was a very large man. He weighed over two hundred pounds; the earth actually shook when he hit. If I hadn't jumped out of the way at the last second, he would have nailed me."

Carrington bounced once and came to rest in the lower branches of a tree, after falling approximately 150 feet. Lev sent a student down to the Jenny Lake boat dock to summon help, then rushed to Carrington's side, where he was soon joined by a student trained as an emergency medical technician. Carrington, severely injured about the head, lacked any vital signs. One by one, Bridwell's clients rappelled down from their ledge in the Hole. The first to reach the ground was the victim's brother-in-law, James McLaughlin, and Lev was forced to break the news to him: Ed Carrington, his neck apparently snapped by the fall, was dead.

At the time of the accident, Carrington, like all Exum clients, had been wearing a Culp Alpine Harness manufactured by Chouinard Equipment Ltd., a standard climbing harness with no previous reputation for problems. Immediately after Carrington fell, Bridwell rappelled down from the top of the route to join his stunned students in the Hole. As he swung from the face into the alcove, he caught sight of Carrington's empty harness still dangling from the rope. He pulled the harness into the Hole after him, examined it for a moment, then dropped it onto the ledge with a curse. The harness was intact, but the strap that should have been secured around Carrington's waist had slipped completely through the metal friction buckle during his second fall, dropping him without warning. This was particularly shocking because the Culp harness had been specifically designed to work even in the event of buckle failure. If the harness is used correctly, the knotted end of the climbing rope rather than the buckle itself is primarily responsible for keeping the ends of the belt mated securely; the harness should have held Carrington even if he'd failed to fasten the strap through the buckle.

What was to gnaw at Bridwell—and to puzzle the scores of National Park Service rangers, Exum guides, Chouinard personnel, attorneys, and insurance adjusters who would investigate the accident over the months to come—was why Carrington had not been tied in correctly. A single glance at the harness as it swung at the mouth of the Hole told Bridwell what had escaped his notice during the course of the climb: Carrington had not tied in as he had been painstakingly taught earlier in the day. The rope, instead of being threaded directly through the harness tie-in loops as specified by the manufacturer, had been tied to a locking carabiner, which in turn had been clipped to the waist strap of the harness—a simpler, faster method that made the integrity of the harness wholly dependent on the integrity of the buckle. As the initial shock of the fatality began to subside and finger-pointing commenced in earnest, when—and why—Carrington had attached the rope to his harness in this hazardous fashion were questions for which a great many people were eager to find answers.

As one might imagine, more than a few of those people were lawyers. On August 22, 1988, exactly two years after the accident—and a day before the statute of limitations was due to expire—the Houston law firm that had employed Carrington brought suit against Bridwell, the Exum school, and Chouinard Equipment on behalf of Rosa Carrington, the victim's widow.

Because the harness had obviously been misused, the case against Chouinard, on the face of it, seemed shaky at best. Exum, the oldest and perhaps most respected company of climbing guides in North America, had suffered only two previous fatalities in its fifty-five-year history (and none at all since 1964) despite logging approximately 3,000 client-days annually—a remarkable safety record that appeared to stack the legal deck in Exum's favor as well. If one was looking for a fall guy to feed to the plaintiff's attorneys, Jim Bridwell seemed to be the leading candidate.

A number of figures in the American climbing community felt that Bridwell did not deserve to be a scapegoat. "A client can't simply switch off his brain because he's being guided up a climb," argues a longtime professional guide who prefers to remain anonymous. "In the end there's only so much a guide can do to counter a client's acts of carelessness."

(Indeed, on a guided ascent in the Tetons in 1967, an act of carelessness by this author nearly resulted in an accident very similar to Carrington's. I was thirteen years old, had graduated from the Exum intermediate rock-climbing class two days before, and was being led up the Grand Teton by a guide named Greg Lowe. I had been carefully tutored, but on this particular morning, I botched up the bowline around my waist, and the knot came untied high on the peak, midway up the crux pitch. I was able to work my way down to a belay ledge and retrieve the rope without falling, and suffered nothing more than an impassioned chewing-out from Lowe, but the consequences of my sloppy knotcraft could just as easily have been terminal.)

In the other camp, Rosa Carrington's lawyers at Fisher, Gallagher, Perrin & Lewis maintained that even if Carrington had incorrectly attached the rope to his harness, Bridwell should have caught the error and rectified it. They said Bridwell, as a professional guide, had no duty more important than ensuring that Carrington—a rank beginner who had been introduced to technical rock climbing only the day before in an Exum basic rock-climbing class—was correctly tied in at all times. Indeed, the Exum Guides Manual plainly and repeatedly admonishes the guides to "check all knots." Bridwell has insisted all along, however, that just prior to the fatal climb he did indeed check to see that Carrington was correctly tied in, with his harness securely fastened.

Bridwell's defenders have advanced the theory that at some point during the ascent—most likely on the belay ledge after the first pitch—Carrington untied without Bridwell's knowledge, perhaps in order to urinate. He then could have hurriedly reattached the rope to the harness incorrectly, using the quickie carabiner system that one of Carrington's companions speculated he'd learned during a guided ascent of Mount Rainier in 1984. This theory is certainly plausible, but it is weakened by the fact that one of the group remembers Carrington relieving himself immediately prior to the Hole in the Wall climb, making it unlikely that he would have done so again only a few minutes later. None of his classmates, in fact, recalled him doing so.

Regardless of when or why Carrington changed his tie-in, the fact remains that he would have gotten away with this quick-and-dirty carabiner attachment method—a method that many climbers employ, with care, in special situations without fearing for their lives—had he fastened the buckle of his harness correctly. By themselves, neither the improperly fastened buckle nor the unorthodox tie-in would have killed him, but the two errors in conjunction sealed Carrington's fate.

Bridwell had worked as a professional mountain guide for the better part of two decades without incident; a wealth of

evidence suggested that he was an able teacher and a consci-
entious, even conservative guide. Nevertheless, his supporters
worried that the Admiral might find himself facing an image
problem, thanks to an article in the May 8, 1986, issue of *Rolling Stone*, which presented him as something of a dissolute
thrill junkie. At one point in the article, Bridwell enthusiastically spoke of an experience he'd had with a UFO. At another,
climber John Long—a well-known Bridwell protégé—
described his mentor as "an occasional abuser of everything,
including himself." Such an image, they feared, would not
serve their friend well when it came time for him to stand
before a jury of Rotarians and housewives.

Once word of the Carrington lawsuits spread, conventional
wisdom in the American climbing community held that
Bridwell would probably wind up taking most of the rap for
the accident, with some of it spilling over to the Exum school
simply for being Bridwell's employer. When I phoned Larry
Boyd, Rosa Carrington's attorney, in March of this year, I was
thus surprised to hear him say that he didn't think Bridwell
and Exum were primarily to blame. "The real culprit," he
declared, "is the company that designed such an unreasonably
dangerous climbing harness."

Whatever the legal merits of Boyd's case against Chouinard,
cynics were quick to point out that Chouinard's were the only
"deep pockets" around. Bridwell was virtually penniless, and
the assets of the Exum school amounted to little more than
a few dozen ropes, a typewriter, and a locker full of climbing
hardware. Chouinard Equipment, on the other hand, took in
$6 million annually in gross receipts and could in theory be
linked by a clever attorney to Yvon Chouinard's clothing company, Patagonia, Inc., a $100 million cash cow. When a poten-
tial liability claim exists and even the faint scent of that kind
of money is on the breeze, lawyers for the plaintiff are going to
sit up and take notice.

Yvon Chouinard, a legendary rock and ice climber in his own right, literally built his equipment business piece by piece. In 1957, after three years of climbing using the primitive hardware of the era, he taught himself blacksmithing, figuring he could supply himself and his friends with better pitons and carabiners than those that were commercially available. He sold the pitons out of his car for $1.50 apiece—five times what European pitons cost, but climbers gradually came to appreciate that his were stronger and better designed, and they were soon buying them as fast as Chouinard could make them. In 1966, Chouinard Equipment opened for business in a tin shed, fondly known as the Skunkworks, next to an abandoned slaughterhouse in Ventura. Receipts totaled about $3,000 that year, but sales doubled the next year and for four years after that.

The company owed its early successes to its cutting-edge design and high quality of material and construction. But pieces of Chouinard hardware, most often crampons or ice axes, occasionally broke during use. Since Chouinard did extensive product testing even back then, his products probably broke less than his competitors', but scores, maybe hundreds of his products did fail. Although no climbers died as a result of poorly made Chouinard gear, more than a few were injured. Yet no lawsuits were filed. Climbers, in those innocent days, simply accepted a certain rate of equipment failure as one of the intrinsic hazards of the game—like avalanches or sudden electrical storms—and prepared for it by carrying an extra ice ax on ice climbs and backing-up belay anchors whenever possible. In 1979, while I was soloing a frozen waterfall a long, long way off the deck, a Chouinard crampon broke and fell off my boot. It was an extremely serious situation. I got myself out of it, but I was predictably upset and fired off an angry letter to Chouinard Equipment. Nevertheless, when the company, unbidden, sent back a replacement part that enabled me to bolt the broken crampon back together, I considered the matter closed. *Wow*, I remember thinking gratefully at the time, *they didn't even charge me for it.*

Not long after that, Chouinard established the most sophisticated quality-control program in the industry, virtually eliminating equipment breakage. It was ironic, therefore, that in March 1986, a window washer in Atlanta named Gilmer MacDougald brought a product liability suit against the company, the first in Chouinard's twenty-nine years in business. Even more ironic, the equipment in question, a locking carabiner, had in no way failed to perform as intended. MacDougald had fallen from high on the side of a building after improperly twisting down the sleeve that locks the carabiner gate in place, and he was severely injured. His suit claimed the design of the device was "defective and unsafe for its intended use."

Anyone unfamiliar with the baroque workings of American jurisprudence might assume that MacDougald's case against Chouinard would simply be thrown out of court. But, lately, sweeping changes in the interpretation of tort law—the law of accidents and personal injury—have made the outcome of liability suits exceedingly unpredictable. Liability law was intended to protect workers, consumers, and accident victims, but the changes have made it profoundly easier for anyone to sue. The authors of the laws may have had noble motives, but the result is a $300 billion annual drain on the U.S. economy that may benefit no one so much as the lawyers involved. Product liability cases multiplied 400 percent between 1976 and 1986, and plaintiffs are now twice as likely to win as they were twenty years ago. The average judgment has grown from $50,000 in the early sixties to more than $250,000 today, and awards greater than $1 million have become commonplace.

Unwilling to take its chances with the courts in this kind of legal climate, Chouinard's insurance company settled the MacDougald claim out of court for $350,000. A second lawsuit hit in March 1988. In August of that same year, the Carrington claim was filed, and three more liability suits followed in quick succession. As the lawsuits mounted, Chouinard Equipment's insurance premiums skyrocketed: for $2 million in coverage—with a $200,000 deductible clause—Chouinard was forced to pay $325,000 a year, an increase of 1,625 percent since 1984.

Although Patagonia, as a separate corporate entity, continued to make money hand over fist, Chouinard Equipment had never been more than marginally profitable at best, and the new insurance burden threatened to drive the hardware company's books into the red. According to Peter Metcalf, Chouinard Equipment's general manager, "In December 1989 our policy was going to be up for renewal, and it looked like it might go up yet again, to five hundred thousand dollars a year, if indeed we could even get insurance at all."

Of the six liability claims made against Chouinard, three could be attributed to blatant misuse of carabiners by non-climbers (a plumber, a roofer, and the aforementioned window washer). The other three claims, the Carrington suit among them, involved improper use of the Culp Alpine Harness, which by now had been taken off the market. Defending these lawsuits became doubly uncertain, thanks to a videotape produced by one of Chouinard's competitors—a tape that, shortly after the Carrington claim was filed, began to circulate through the climbing underground like a piece of scandalously exotic pornography.

The handiwork of John Bouchard—the maverick, outspoken owner of Wild Things, a New Hampshire–based outlet for cutting-edge climbing gear—the video graphically depicted the buckle and waist belt of a Chouinard harness (a more recent model than the Culp harness, without designated tie-in loops, but with essentially the same buckle design) coming undone in a laboratory test situation. Bouchard—who was himself facing a product liability suit of dubious merit when he made the tape—says that the video was not intended for public consumption and that the last thing he wanted to do was compound Chouinard's legal woes. Rather, Bouchard insists, the video was meant to be a shot across the bow of complacent associates in the climbing business, to shock people into realizing that defensive action needed to be taken by the industry as a whole.

Whatever Bouchard's motives, the video did nothing to lessen Chouinard's problems. Were it to be admitted as evidence at a trial, it could be damning. Which was unfortunate, because although the buckle in the video did indeed let go under body weight, it failed under conditions that would, in the view of most climbers (Bouchard notwithstanding), be all but impossible to duplicate on an actual climb—and absolutely impossible to duplicate on the Culp harness if the tie-in loops were used as intended.

Such subtleties, however, were likely to be lost on a non-climbing judge or jury. "The plaintiff would pay five hundred dollars a day to some professor of engineering—a professional testifier—who'd never been near a climb in his life," explains Jim McCarthy, a New York civil attorney, rock climber, and past president of the American Alpine Club, "and he'd stand up there, introduce himself as an expert, and testify that there's obviously a design defect here. In conjunction with the video, that could be very effective."

As Chouinard's liability predicament intensified, the folks next door at Patagonia began to get nervous. On paper, the two corporations were completely independent, so even if a plaintiff managed to mount a successful suit against the embattled hardware company, he stood little chance of getting his hands on any of Patagonia's bounteous assets. Nonetheless, given the many close ties between Chouinard Equipment and Patagonia, it was at least conceivable that this "corporate veil" could be pierced, and this remote possibility frightened the lawyers representing both corporations.

As time went on, the previously unthinkable looked like the only remaining option: Chouinard Equipment, foundering on the shoals of tort law, would have to be cut loose. On April 17, 1989, Yvon Chouinard's namesake business—the enterprise that had launched his charmed career and profoundly influenced the course of an entire sport—filed for bankruptcy under Chapter 11.

Chapter 11 put all the litigation on hold, buying time for Chouinard to figure out a course of action. In the end, the company was put on the block in federal bankruptcy court, and a group of Chouinard employees led by Metcalf formed an entirely new corporation, christened Black Diamond. Metcalf swung a deal to buy all of Chouinard Equipment's orders, machinery, inventory, and assets "tangible and intangible"— everything, in effect, but the Chouinard name and the company's onerous liabilities.

On December 1, 1989, when Black Diamond assumed ownership, little seemed to change in the company's day-to-day operations. But since the corporation was brand new, with no lawsuits hanging over its head, its liability insurance now cost $150,000 yearly with a $20,000 deductible, instead of $325,000 with a $220,000 deductible.

Chouinard solved his liability problems by getting out of the climbing business altogether. And for those operators who haven't closed up shop, insurance is now actually a little cheaper and a little easier to come by than it was two or three years ago. But the American fondness for bringing lawsuits continues apace. "It's a terrible, pernicious disease as far as I'm concerned," says Jim McCarthy. "People in our society refuse to take responsibility for their own actions. 'It can't be *my* fault, it always has to be someone else's fault.'"

The ramifications of this "pernicious disease" already ripple through the mountaineering industry. The leading American manufacturer of climbing ropes, Blue Water, will no longer sponsor climbing competitions or even donate ropes as prizes for fear that such generosity could invite liability suits. Black Diamond has just invented a unique, quasi-locking carabiner that would solve the problem of gate flutter—a common and potentially very serious phenomenon wherein carabiner gates vibrate open during leader falls—but has been advised by its attorneys not to put it on the market. "It's too innovative," explains Metcalf. "It works beautifully, but it's prone to being misused, so there's no way we can sell it without risking the company."

Such fallout, however, is chicken feed compared with the potential consequences of a liability claim slated to go to trial on May 31 of this year in Cheyenne, Wyoming. McCarthy, who will be testifying on behalf of the National Park Service, worries that it could have draconian repercussions not only for climbers but also for all those who enjoy the wilderness.

On June 28, 1987, four college students working as seasonal employees at Grand Teton National Park scrambled up the east ridge of 11,938-foot Buck Mountain, near the southern end of the Teton Range. During the descent, the party split up. Two of the students made it back down by noon, but another became stranded on a ledge, and the fourth slipped on a hard-frozen snow slope and sustained a massive head injury. He managed to regain consciousness, but stumbled into a pool of shallow meltwater from which he was unable to crawl out. The first two students waited until midafternoon before notifying the authorities, who in turn waited several more hours before mounting a search. The student trapped on the ledge was eventually found and rescued at two thirty in the morning, but the fourth student—still lying in the pool—wasn't located until daybreak, by which time he was long dead from hypothermia. The suit stemming from this incident alleges that the Park Service failed to "adequately regulate recreational climbing activity in Grand Teton National Park" and didn't execute the rescue fast enough.

"The assumption that the Park Service has an obligation to mount a helicopter rescue every time someone is treed or reported missing is simply outrageous," says McCarthy. "If the plaintiff wins this one, you're going to see every national park in the country shut down and closed up."

Don Coelho, a law enforcement specialist for the park, who is in charge of all court and legal action stemming from incidents there, says that McCarthy's alarmist rhetoric is not so far-fetched. "We're all nervous about the outcome. . . . The precedent could be disastrous."*

Climbing used to be a fringe activity grounded in self-reliance and independence—more a close-knit subculture than a conventional sport. Climbers loved the extreme risk, the low-tech equipment, the very antimodernness of the game. The rules demanded commitment and responsibility, and the players learned them from experienced friends and elders, usually through a long apprenticeship. "Climbing wasn't something you just did on weekends," explains Yvon Chouinard. "By God, you understood that you had to dedicate years of your life to learning all its different aspects. Otherwise you stood a good chance of getting killed."

Times have changed. The victim in the Buck Mountain fiasco was a first-time climber. Likewise, the victims in virtually every other mountaineering mishap that's resulted in litigation have had either precious little climbing experience

---

* The United States Court of Appeals, Tenth Circuit, resolved the lawsuit on November 13, 1991, by ruling in favor of the National Park Service.

or none at all. In part, this could be attributed to the sport's recent explosive growth, due mainly to the emphasis placed on a relatively new facet known as sport climbing: ascending short, steep cliffs, or even artificial walls, equipped with bomb-proof, tightly spaced, pre-placed anchors. It's made the sport easier to learn—and more accessible. For the first time ever, climbing is being aggressively marketed—in some cases by the same climbers who speak of the good old days—and packaged almost as a mainstream sport: thrilling but not particularly life-threatening.

To pick up the sport, many would-be climbers turn to guide services and climbing schools, assuming that their instructor will be infallible: a steel-hard semi-deity possessed of unerring mountain savvy—precisely the image that guides themselves want to project and indeed take great pains to project. Guide services (and equipment companies), after all, are first and foremost businesses, and as such they resort to much the same hyperbolic language and marketing strategies that other busi-nesses employ. In unguarded moments, mountaineering com-panies will—or used to—admit as much. When, for example, I wrote to Chouinard Equipment in 1979 complaining about my broken crampon, I included a page from the latest Chouinard catalogue, which boasted of the unparalleled workmanship and dependability of the product. In reply, I got an apologetic note from an employee who confessed, "Hey, you know how it is: Advertising and bullshit go together like peanut butter and jelly, like hot dogs and mustard, like Ginger Rogers and Fred Astaire."

Nowadays, the promotional brochures and catalogues of guide services and hardware manufacturers do include dis-claimers: detailed legal boilerplate warning of the hazards of climbing. But the stilted language leaves one with the impres-sion that the disclaimers are mere legal formalities (what law-yers refer to as "flypaper") and thus are not intended to be taken seriously—an impression reinforced by the pages and pages of cheerful catalogue copy that inevitably follow.

"In a sense," says Michael Kennedy, an experienced mountaineer and the editor of *Climbing* magazine, "guide services and gear manufacturers have helped bring the liability crisis on themselves by underplaying the sport's dangers in their marketing. They know they're going to have a tough time selling people on climbing if the first thing they tell them is 'You stand a good chance of getting killed.' As a consequence, people take up climbing thinking it's just another form of recreation, without being tuned into its traditions, its spiritual side. Then, surprised when they get hurt, like good Americans they sue somebody."

The current liability problem is not without practical responses, however. One thing companies could do to discourage future suits is refuse to settle current ones out of court. "A huge number of lawsuits are filed with little or no merit," explains McCarthy. "But they're expensive to defend, climbing sounds exotic, the insurance company wants the hell out of there, so there's a fat settlement. And the plaintiff's attorney walks away with his one-third, no problem, ready to do it all over again next time."

Most heads of climbing-related businesses agree, at least in principle, that it would be much better for the industry as a whole if each and every liability claim were fought through the courts. But for all the tough talk, thus far the only company that has actually stuck to the hard line and refused to settle has been John Bouchard's Wild Things. Yvon Chouinard, when asked why he was so quick to settle out of court, asserts that insurance companies are to blame: "As soon as you buy insurance, you surrender the right to decide whether to fight a case or not. They insist on making that decision."

Perhaps the best way for a company to avoid being sued, suggests Chouinard, is "simply to stay small, to keep it in your backyard, like I started out. The trick is, you don't carry any insurance, you figure out a way to keep your assets out of the business, and nobody will be interested in suing you. And if somebody does sue you, you just walk away from it. But you have to make sure you don't get greedy, because as soon as you get big, you become a target."

Of course, schools and equipment manufacturers might also reconsider how they sell climbing to the American public. Climbing has marketed so successfully against its dangerous image that the beginner has come to believe that by plunking down his charge card at a reputable climbing school he is buying expertise and safety—that at his level of the game, at least, climbing is fun and maybe scary, but never deadly.

The sale of Chouinard Equipment did not make the lawsuits disappear. In early April, the Carrington case was scheduled to go to trial in June or July. However, since Chouinard Equipment declared bankruptcy, piercing the corporate veil has become considerably more problematic. Insiders expected that by the time you read this article the claim will have been settled out of court.

Meanwhile, profits are still piling up in the coffers of Patagonia, Inc. Exum has yet to settle its suit—a suit kept alive, according to Rosa Carrington's family, at the insistence of Ed Carrington's old law firm—but is conducting business as usual. Jim Bridwell, who has settled out of court, is presently climbing and guiding in Southern California.*

And Ed Carrington, of course, is still dead. No obvious culprit has emerged from the legal fracas, and people still ask why Carrington—taught by a top-notch instructor at a highly respected school using the finest equipment made—is not alive today.

A satisfactory answer to that question will never be forth-

---

* Jim Bridwell died on February 16, 2018, at the age of seventy-three.

coming. The most that can be said with any certainty is that someone made a small, innocent mistake—or more likely still, several people made a series of small, innocent mistakes. And climbing, for better or worse, has always been a game in which the penalty for even a single, apparently tiny error is often considerably more than anyone wants to pay.

GATES OF THE ARCTIC

The route climbed to a high divide that was notched like a gunsight between bald granite cliffs. Humping a big load up the pass, I was preoccupied with the weight biting into my shoulders and the rocks shifting underfoot, so I didn't see the bear until it was less than 75 yards away. I paused to catch my breath, glanced up, and there he was: a 350-pound grizzly, loping across the talus that spilled down from the notch. Because the wind was at the bear's back he hadn't yet noticed me, but a single route led over the divide, and I was smack in the animal's path.

As grizzlies go, it was a relatively small one. His bulk would have dwarfed any lineman in the NFL, however, and the beast's dull, tiny eyes did not convey congenial intent. I was deep in the Alaskan Brooks Range, well north of the Arctic Circle, so there were no trees for me to climb. I didn't have a gun. Running, I knew, might invite attack. Too scared to breathe, I tried to remain calm but felt my mouth go dry.

The bear kept coming. At thirty yards, catching my scent, he stopped abruptly and reared onto his hind legs. His shaggy blond fur rippled in the breeze. His arms were as thick as spruce logs. Stories of gruesome bear maulings fast-forwarded through my brain. The grizzly sniffed the air, stared at me, sniffed some more. And then he dropped to all fours and bolted in the opposite direction, sprinting across a jumble of tank-trap boulders at a speed that defied belief.

PUBLISHED IN *SMITHSONIAN*, JUNE 1995

The date was July 2, 1974. Two decades later, the memory is still vivid. For a long time after the bear ran off, I sat on a rock and just listened to the pounding of my heart. It was an hour after midnight. Mosquitoes swarmed around my face. Far above the divide, a prow of jagged granite burned orange in the twilight, illuminated by a sun that never set. Ranks of nameless mountains marched into the distance as far as I could see.

Over the preceding weeks I'd become attuned to wolf song and the whistle of golden plovers, walked through a snorting tide of caribou, gazed down from untrod summits, gorged on fat grayling pulled from crystalline streams. And now I'd stared into the eyes of *Ursus arctos horribilis*, only to discover that the star of my nightmares was even more discombobulated by the encounter than I was. I would see four more grizzlies before the month was out.

I'd climbed and fished in the emptiest reaches of the American West, but Alaska made the wilds of the Lower 48 seem insipid and tame, a toothless simulacrum. In the Arctic, for the first time in my life I was surrounded by real wilderness. Even as a callow twenty-year-old, I understood that such an experience, in the late twentieth century, was a rare and wondrous privilege.

Six years later, in 1980, the United States Congress recognized the singularity of the Brooks Range and set aside eight and a half million acres of it as Gates of the Arctic National Park and Preserve. A vast sprawl of wilderness the size of Massachusetts and Connecticut combined, Gates is the second-largest unit in our national park system, yet few Americans have ever heard of it, and fewer still have actually been there: Gates is visited by some 2,000 people a year, compared to the 9.3 million who visit Great Smoky Mountains National Park, or the 3.8 million who visit Yosemite.

This gaping disparity is largely a function of access. Yosemite lies three hours by automobile from San Francisco Bay and the region's 3 million residents; tourists can gawk at Half Dome, El Capitan, and Yosemite Falls without ever stepping out of their air-conditioned cars. Although Gates of the Arctic has scenery that rivals Yosemite—and eleven times as much acreage— Gates is situated in remote northern Alaska. It's impossible to drive through Gates, because the park has no roads. Within the park boundaries, moreover, there are no ranger stations, no motels, no snack bars, no souvenir shops, no maintained campgrounds, no facilities of any kind. Except for widely scattered game trails, there aren't even any footpaths.

The park's administrators do not consider the absence of amenities to be a shortcoming. In the opinion of the National Park Service, rather, the fact that Gates is a hard place to get to, and even harder to get around in, is its saving grace. Park regulations have been formulated to keep development and visitation to a bare minimum.

Not everyone is pleased with this policy. Critics carp that Gates is an "elitist" park. What's the point of setting aside such an immense tract of land, they ask, if it's effectively off-limits to all but a tiny handful of the American public?

The answer, explains John M. Kauffmann, a now-retired civil servant who was in charge of planning the park in the 1970s, is that "the northern environment is easy to damage and slow to heal. Human impact is felt much more strongly than in temperate latitudes." Some arctic lichens grow less than a sixteenth of an inch annually. A hiker's footsteps can leave divots in the tundra that take forty years to grow back. The passage of a single all-terrain vehicle is apt to scar the muskeg for centuries. "When we were planning the park," says Kauffmann, "we realized that this was America's last big chunk of raw wilderness. There would never be any more. If Gates of the Arctic were to be made as accessible as Yosemite, the very things that make it worth preserving would be destroyed."

In his book, *Alaska's Brooks Range*, Kauffmann writes that when deciding how much development should be permitted in Gates, he and the other planners quickly determined that it would be best "to do absolutely nothing":

> *Draw a protective boundary and leave the place alone: no roads, no trails, no bridges, no campgrounds, no interpretive signs, none of the woodsy aids and conveniences with which most parks are equipped. They would change the character and the quality of the land. Visitors would take the Brooks Range on its terms, not theirs. We borrowed a karate term to call it a black-belt park. Not for neophytes, it would be at the ascetic end of a spectrum of national parks, with no one park needing to be all things to all people. We remembered Aldo Leopold's comment, "I am glad I shall never be young without wild country to be young in. Of what avail are forty freedoms without a blank spot on the map?"*

Thanks to aerial cartography and satellite navigation, alas, there are no more blank spots on any map, not even in the Arctic. Every year more people troop through Gates. The National Park Service has estimated that by 2010, the annual tally of visitors will swell to 18,000—an absurdly small number by the standards of other parks, but a ninefold increase over current visitation. Some environmental advocates, Kauffmann among them, believe many of the park's most extraordinary attractions have already been irreparably damaged by excessive use. Last summer, curious about how "America's last big chunk of raw wilderness" was holding up, I returned to the same part of the Brooks Range I visited in 1974.

I embark for the backcountry, like most people who visit Gates, from the metropolis of Bettles, population thirty-three, twenty-five miles outside the park's boundary. Twenty years earlier, there had been a single bush pilot in town; now there are three competing air-taxi services employing a half-dozen pilots. Accompanied by Alaskan friends Roman and Peggy Dial, I climb into a 1956 de Havilland Beaver moored on the Koyukuk River. Pilot Jay Jespersen opens the throttle, the airplane's aluminum floats lurch free of the roiling current, and we fly north by northwest under a lowering sky.

Two hours out of Bettles, we bank hard over a small lake. Jay scans for moose or other obstacles, brings the Beaver down, and we wade ashore in a light rain. As the airplane flies off, the roar of its engine reverberates from the surrounding peaks, quickly fades, and is replaced by a monumental silence. I feel a long way from anywhere. In fact, we're closer to Siberia than Anchorage or Juneau. The nearest highway is the haul road for the trans-Alaska oil pipeline, 140 miles to the east. Grinning like a thief, I shoulder my pack and follow Peggy across the tundra.

The lake where we landed is the source of the Alatna, one of the major rivers draining the Brooks Range. For the initial leg of our three-week Arctic ramble, we intend to paddle forty-seven miles downriver, but the mighty Alatna begins as an ankle-deep trickle, so our inflatable rafts remain in our backpacks and we walk until the river becomes deep enough to float.

The Alatna flows down a broad U-shaped valley bounded by rubbly escarpments rising into the clouds. Clumps of caribou—two hundred here, seventy-five there—file slowly across the stark terrain. From the air, the valley had looked as smooth and manicured as a golf course, but it turns out to be the typical swamp of tussock tundra. The valley bottom is covered with millions of spongy, cauliflower-shaped mounds of cotton grass, twenty inches high, which make for slow, frustrating travel. One must either high-step over each mound, which necessitates walking in the sucking bog from which the cotton grass grows, or stride uncertainly from crown to tippy tussock crown, inviting pratfalls and twisted ankles.

To escape the tussocks we search out gravel bars along the river, wading back and forth across the stream to link them. Everywhere the damp sand is imprinted with the tracks of caribou, moose, wolf—and bear. Comparing my size 9 boot to a fresh grizzly print, I estimate the bruin would wear size 20 Nikes.

Roman, and especially Peggy, share my "bearanoia," as she calls it. In 1986, Roman walked, skied, and paddled a thousand miles from one end of the Brooks Range to the other, and Peggy, pregnant with their first child, accompanied him for a month of the journey. Near the headwaters of the Nahtuk River, a tributary of the Alatna, they surprised a grizzly sow foraging among the blueberry bushes. Unlike the bear I'd met in 1974, which immediately ran away, this one bluff-charged them repeatedly.

"Bears have poor eyesight, so they'll bluff-charge in order to see how you react," says Roman, a peripatetic professor of biology at Alaska Pacific University. "If you act like prey and run, they'll assume that's what you are." Somehow maintaining their composure, Peggy and Roman edged away from the grizzly's turf as nonchalantly as possible, and after charging four times, the bear left them alone.

On this trip I'm carrying a weapon to defend against bear attack, the first time I've ever done so: an aerosol can of pepper spray of the sort urbanites use to ward off muggers. Additionally, Roman has a small handgun. Back in Bettles, I showed my pepper spray to a bush pilot named Barry Yoseph. "Yeah," he pronounced as soon as he stopped laughing, "I reckon them bears will be mighty pleased to see you carrying that stuff. Should add a little spice to their supper." The pilot was only slightly less disdainful of Roman's revolver. "You think that little toy is gonna slow a bear down? Only handgun with enough pop to put a bullet through a grizzly's skull is one of these here," he'd insisted, unholstering a giant .44 Magnum like the one Clint Eastwood made famous in *Dirty Harry*.

Yoseph's comments weigh heavily on my mind as I walk past an embankment where a grizzly has dug up a parka squirrel den. The excavation, which is recent and extensive, looks like the work of a backhoe gone berserk.

After we've covered four miles on foot, the Alatna becomes marginally deep enough to float our tiny rafts. We only have two blow-up boats for the three of us, so Roman and Peggy share one, and I take most of the gear in the other. It's a pleasure to let the river propel us, but shortly after casting off, the Dials rip a hole in the bottom of their overloaded craft, forcing us to stop and make camp on a gravel bar where we can dry the boat over a willow fire and patch the leak.

By morning, the rain clouds are gone. It's only August 5, but the air already has a sharp autumnal bite. Lazing around camp until noon, we sip coffee in the muted sunlight and watch the underwater antics of small wren-like birds called dippers. When we get under way, feeder creeks rapidly bolster the Alatna's volume, transforming it into a flume of whitewater that carries us south at three times our walking speed, with scandalously little effort.

Within an hour of breaking camp, we reach the vanguard of the northern tree line, a single puny spruce resembling an overgrown pipe cleaner, and soon thereafter scrubby northern forest known as taiga (a Russian term meaning "land of little sticks") crowds the shore. The Arctic sun scribes a low arc across the sky, never climbing much higher than the horizon, casting the denuded bluffs above the valley in a spectral glow. When we pitch the tent at day's end, we have paddled more than forty miles.

Twenty years earlier, six friends and I spent thirty-two days in the Brooks Range without seeing another soul. In the morning I am thus taken aback to see a group of ten people camped across the river. Before the day is out, moreover, a yellow Cessna disgorges two additional planeloads of wilderness seekers on a nearby lake.

The Alatna, like most big rivers in the Brooks Range, flows fast but has no rapids more challenging than Class 2 riffles (on a scale of 1 to 6). If the rugged terrain and absence of trails make hiking through this country a labor-intensive grind, waterborne travel is downright cushy. Which explains why the great majority of visitors to Gates of the Arctic flock to the half-dozen navigable rivers—and why, in a park with so much acreage and so few humans, those visitors are often dismayed to encounter other people.

I'm disappointed, too, although I shouldn't be surprised. Before we'd left Bettles, chief ranger Glenn Sherrill warned, "You can hike through 99 percent of Gates and I guarantee you won't see anyone. But park use is heavily concentrated along the Alatna, the Noatak, the John, and the North Fork of the Koyukuk. If you're looking for solitude, stay away from these rivers. The only other place you're likely to run into a crowd is in the Arrigetch."

The Arrigetch Peaks, a cluster of sheer granite spires west of the Alatna Valley, comprise one of the loveliest places in Gates of the Arctic, if not the world. Hence its relative popularity, although the "crowd" to which Sherrill referred amounts to no more than 50 to 150 people annually in the entire 150-square-mile Arrigetch massif. "Down in Utah, where I was a ranger until transferring to Alaska two years ago," Sherrill mused, "a number that small would effectively be considered zero use. In Gates we consider it extremely heavy use."

Fifty or a hundred visitors a year is a problem in the Arrigetch because in the High Arctic, that many people, no matter how careful, are bound to leave an indelible mark on the landscape. Not very many years ago, the trudge up Arrigetch Creek demanded attentive route-finding and nasty bushwhacking through all-but-impenetrable alder thickets. Now the march of boots has trampled a muddy thoroughfare up most of the lower valley. At popular campsites, the tundra has been worn down to bare earth. Bears in the area have grown habituated to human offal, prompting rangers to place steel barrels at the busiest camps so that the bruins won't pilfer backpackers' food and garbage.

As Peggy, Roman, and I hike up Arrigetch Creek from its confluence with the Alatna, though, we encounter nobody. Halfway up the valley the makeshift trail we've been following peters out, and we see no further sign of human passage whatsoever.

The higher we ascend, the more the country resembles the phantasmal scenery of a Tolkien novel. Our route takes us across soft carpets of reindeer lichen beneath sinister black cliffs and hanging glaciers. The creek, opaque with glacial sediment, is never far away. Most of the time the stream is a thundering cascade, frothing from drop to drop over gargantuan blocks of stone; at other places it slows and spreads into placid cerulean pools in which reflections of the surrounding alps shimmer like hallucinations.

At the head of Arrigetch Creek, we find ourselves in a natural cul-de-sac, nearly encircled by soaring vertical walls. We continue the only way possible: by going up and over the top—a climb of 4,000 vertical feet that culminates on an airy summit as slender as a thorn. The whole expanse of the Arrigetch is visible from this vantage, a dazzling chaos of mile-high granite pickets. As we descend to the west, into a virginal cirque cradling a half-frozen lake, I am reminded that it is the astonishing *wildness* of this place, even more than its splendor, that is responsible for the bittersweet rapture expanding in my chest.

A mere two-day walk (albeit a strenuous one) from the

relative hubbub along the Alatna has transported us into a landscape as primeval as that which moved Bob Marshall so powerfully six decades ago. Describing the country east of the Alatna, the celebrated conservationist wrote: "Nothing I had ever seen, Yosemite or the Grand Canyon or Mt. McKinley rising from the Susitna, had given me such a sense of immensity. . . . No sight or sound or smell or feeling even remotely hinted of men or their creations. It seemed as if time had dropped away a million years and we were back in a primordial world."

Marshall wasn't the first Caucasian to penetrate the Brooks Range—navy lieutenant George M. Stoney noted the "rugged, weather-scarred peaks, lofty minarets [and] cathedral spires" of the Arrigetch while exploring the Alatna as early as 1886—but Marshall was the Arctic's most ardent champion. He is responsible for the name, Gates of the Arctic, which he bestowed upon a pair of stately mountains bracketing the North Fork of the Koyukuk. Park planner John Kauffmann observed that Marshall's appellation has "captured the imagination of all who have heard it. It did much to bring about national park status for the area."

For millennia before Marshall or Stoney ever set foot in Alaska, of course, Athapaskan (Indian) and Nunamiut (inland Eskimo) hunter-gatherers lived and traveled throughout the Brooks Range. According to an oral history passed down over the centuries, the Nunamiut people were created by a giant deity named Aiyagomahala. After giving them life, he taught the Nunamiut to live off the land, and showed them how to survive the brutal cold and long night of the Arctic winter.

So that he and his teachings would be remembered, Aiyagomahala set one of his gloves down beside the Alatna River and transformed it into the most spectacular cordillera in the Brooks Range, the peaks now rising around me. The

Nunamiut christened them the Arrigich, which in English means "fingers of the hand extended."

Prior to 1890, bands of Nunamiut roamed across much of what is now Gates of the Arctic National Park. Contact with white explorers and whalers at the turn of the century, however, introduced epidemics of measles and influenza for which the natives had no immunity. During this same period, the teeming herds of caribou that provided them with most of their food, clothing, and shelter went into cyclical decline. Ravaged by famine and disease, the surviving Nunamiut migrated from the mountains, their traditional homeland, to settlements on the Arctic coast. By the time of Marshall's first trip to the Arctic, in 1929, they had all but vanished from the central Brooks Range.

Today the Nunamiut are back in Gates of the Arctic. Most of those who live within the park reside in the village of Anaktuvuk Pass, a settlement of plywood shacks and prefab homes huddled on a broad windswept divide near the source of the John River. There are no flush toilets in this community of 250 (the permafrost makes plumbing problematic), but there is electricity, cable television, a handful of telephones, a fancy new school—and an astonishing number of automobiles, given that there is nowhere to drive beyond the few blocks of gravel streets that comprise downtown Anaktuvuk.

Village existence is an incongruous blend of the timeless and the modern. A wage-based economy has supplanted the subsistence life of old to a great degree, but hunting and trapping remain an extremely important component of Nunamiut culture. On occasion, this has led to conflict with the National Park Service.

The Nunamiut have forced the Park Service to rethink some of its fundamental policies. Initially, Kauffmann explains, the agency was inclined to regard Gates as it regarded parks in

the Lower 48, "where the rules were clear and long established, hunting, even for subsistence, was out of the question,
and native people were usually artifacts of the past rather
than a living part of the ecosystem." In Gates, however, park
administrators had to make concessions to Alaskan politics,
native traditions, and idiosyncrasies of the northern lifestyle.
Ultimately, the Alaska National Interest Lands Conservation
Act of 1980 (ANILCA) decreed that subsistence hunting and
trapping would be permitted in the park by natives and non-
natives alike.

Conservationists are unhappy about this and other aspects
of ANILCA. In a questionable interpretation of the regulations, subsistence hunters drive all-terrain vehicles through
Gates with impunity. Miles of ruts made by eight-wheeled
amphibious machines known as Argos now crisscross the tundra around Anaktuvuk Pass and scar several valleys across the
northeast quadrant of the park.

A controversial compromise was hammered out between
the Nunamiut and the Park Service in the summer of 1994 that
promises to contain the environmental damage done by ATVs.
The deal rearranges park wilderness boundaries, allowing the
use of ATVs in 200,000 acres of ancestral hunting grounds but
prohibiting mechanized access beyond these mutually recognized areas.

ATV tracks are nowhere in evidence on the back side of the
Arrigetch massif, in any case, where Peggy, Roman, and I are
camped in the rain at the foot of a mountain that looks like
an Arctic version of Yosemite's Half Dome. The terrain here,
like most of the higher reaches of the Brooks Range, is much
too rugged for Argos, and few hikers wander this far from the
navigable rivers. The only tracks we've seen belong to caribou,
Dall sheep, and bears.

"For dinner tonight, how about potato flakes and macaroni?" Roman asks as raindrops drum on the tent fly. "They taste great together."

"That's what you said about the tuna and spaghetti," Peggy replies dubiously. We decide to dine on freeze-dried chili instead.

In the morning, Peggy finds a week-old grizzly kill just beyond camp—the half-eaten carcass of a young caribou. Wondering when the bear will return to eat the rest of it, we try to take our minds off the subject of grizzlies by investigating the glassy chunks of quartz, some as large as household appliances, that lie scattered across the surrounding tundra like pieces of petrified ice.

Striking camp and moving on, we struggle up a steep pass as the storm builds to a howling gale. Twenty years ago, my friends and I scrambled easily over this same pass on a sun-baked 80-degree afternoon. Now horizontal sleet sprays the cliffs that cap the divide, making the rock too slippery to attempt without technical climbing gear. Pulling coils of rope from our packs, we spend the next three hours negotiating a five-hundred-foot precipice, while icy water fills our boots and dribbles down upstretched arms.

On the far side of the pass, shivering uncontrollably and soaked to the skin, we escape the wind but remain in dense fog that restricts visibility to a few dozen yards. Navigating by compass and altimeter, we pick our way through a dream-scape of lush heaths and tortured stone. Waterfalls tumble over sprawling glacier-polished slabs streaked with orange lichens. Massive boulders appear out of the mist, jutting from mead-ows carpeted in heather, moss, and tufted *Dryas* that would put the loveliest Japanese garden to shame.

My feet hurt. My pack feels like it weighs two hundred pounds. I'm bone-tired and dripping wet, and want very badly to stop walking and crawl into my sleeping bag. In forty-eight hours, however, an airplane is scheduled to meet us at a distant lake. If we are to arrive by the appointed day, it is imperative that we keep moving. There is still one more precipitous pass to climb before we can rest.

People who have never ventured into the back beyond might well wonder why anyone would subject himself to such suffering. As we trudge forward on exhausted legs, the answer is everywhere I direct my gaze. The Brooks Range is such a seductive place to visit, moreover, not in spite of the incumbent hardships, but precisely because of them. The fact that admission to this Eden requires a toll paid in sweat, pain, and fear makes its beauty all the more intoxicating.

It's after midnight when we reach the base of the next pass. The slope is steep and the footing loose, but as we push stubbornly upward, the fog lifts, unveiling a panorama of ripsaw mountains in the fading light. Scraps of cloud wrap the summits like gauze. The ghostly blue tongue of a glacier hangs from a nearby ridge. By and by we stand atop the pass, a shank of wind-scoured rock marking the Arctic Divide—the hydrographic apex of the continent. Snowmelt burbling from the cliffs at my back is bound for the Arctic Ocean; ahead, in the valley at my feet, we will camp tonight beside a creek that flows into the Pacific.

I'll be happy as hell to finally make camp. I look forward to a long, sybaritic soak, come tomorrow afternoon, in the hot spring that lies a half-day walk down the valley. But the thought of our impending departure already saddens me. I'm not ready for the trip to be over.

As Bob Marshall wrote six decades ago at the conclusion of an extended Brooks Range sojourn, "In a day I should be in Fairbanks . . . in a week in Seattle and the great, thumping, modern world. I should be living once more among the accumulated accomplishments of man. The world with its present population needs these accomplishments. It cannot live on wilderness, except incidentally and sporadically. Nevertheless, to four human beings, just back from the source streams of the Koyukuk, no comfort, no security, no invention, no brilliant thought which the modern world had to offer could provide half the elation of the days spent in the little-explored, uninhabited world of the Arctic wilderness."

LOVING THEM TO DEATH

The long-distance connection was good, but as Sally Bacon held the phone to her ear in her Phoenix kitchen, she couldn't make sense of what she was hearing. Thirty days earlier, she'd sent her sixteen-year-old son, Aaron, to a Utah-based wilderness school called North Star Expeditions. And now some woman from North Star was telling her, "Aaron is down. We can't get a pulse."

"What does that mean, you can't get a pulse?" Sally inquired, uncomprehending.

"Aaron's been airlifted to the hospital in Page, Arizona," replied the disembodied female voice. "Call your husband. He's been given the hospital phone number." Sally frantically called her spouse, Bob Bacon, at his office; sounding numb, he repeated what he knew: Aaron had apparently collapsed in the desert. It was a freak accident. There was nothing anyone could do. Their son was dead.

On March 1, 1994, the Bacons had enrolled Aaron in a sixty-three-day North Star course conducted in the sandstone badlands of southern Utah, near the small town of Escalante. He was a funny, articulate kid who wrote prizewinning poetry and excelled academically. But early in his sophomore year at Phoenix's Central High School, Aaron started smoking marijuana every day and ditching classes. His grades plummeted. Bob and Sally repeatedly caught him lying to them. He grew increasingly sullen, and succumbed to frequent crying jags.

That January, Aaron—a tall, skinny youth with shoulder-length hair—had been jumped by a gang of Crips in the school parking lot. Although he vehemently denied being a gang-banger, witnesses reported that the Crips called him Rabbit, an apparent gang moniker, and acted as if they knew Aaron well. Sally, an artist and part-time real estate agent, and Bob, an eminent Phoenix architect, worried that he had been buy-ing weed from the Crips, or maybe even selling it to them. "That really scared us," says Sally. "Aaron seemed to be caught in a big downhill spiral." The Bacons decided the time had come to take serious measures.

Two years previously, the Bacons had sent Aaron's older brother, Jarid, to Hazelden, the renowned Minnesota clinic, to be treated for drug addiction. Despite spending thirty days there—at a cost of $20,000—within two weeks of returning home, he started using again. "We didn't think a residential facility like that was best for Aaron," says Sally. "His problems didn't seem as severe as Jarid's. We wanted to try something else first."

From a friend of a friend, Sally had heard about a com-pany called North Star that was reportedly quite successful at turning around troubled adolescents. North Star's program was based on an increasingly popular regimen known as wilderness therapy: a blend of intensive counseling, "tough love," and Spartan hikes through the desert—it sounded to Sally like a cross between the Betty Ford Center and Outward Bound. "Students at North Star Expeditions learn that Mother Nature does not make exceptions," explained the brochure she received in the mail. "They learn responsibility, self-discipline, and motivation."

Tuition for the two-month program was $13,900, plus another $775 if the Bacons wished to have Aaron "escorted" to Escalante by North Star personnel, which the company

strongly recommended. Bob's design and consulting business, once prosperous, had lately been teetering on the brink
of insolvency, and the Bacons no longer had that kind of cash
at their disposal. But after talking to the owners of North Star
and several parents whose kids had been helped by the program, says Sally, "we were given a lot of hope that North Star
was going to build Aaron's self-esteem. I knew it would be
rigorous, but I pictured him out there with God and nature,
hiking all day, discussing his issues with therapists around the
campfire at night. I thought it would be perfect for him."

Still, the Bacons had concerns, which they expressed during
a long meeting at a Phoenix hotel with Lance and Barbara Jaggar, two of North Star's owners. "I was worried because Aaron
was very, very thin," says Sally, "but Barbara assured me, 'Oh,
we would never let any of our students lose weight.'"

Bob warned the Jaggars that Aaron didn't respond favorably
to intimidation. "Don't worry," insisted Lance, a 280-pound
former military policeman with an imposing mien and a neck
like a fire hydrant. "I have a special gift for working with kids.
They really open up to me." Convinced, Sally and Bob took out
a second mortgage to pay for the course, and, without telling
Aaron, signed him up.

At six A.M. on March 1, Aaron awoke to the sound of the
family's three shar-peis growling outside his bedroom door.
A moment later, his father walked in with Lance Jaggar and
Jaggar's brother-in-law, Don Burkhart. Taking Aaron's arm in
his meaty grip, Jaggar announced, "You're coming with me. If
I detect any resistance, I'll assume you are trying to get away
and I'll take the appropriate action. Do I make myself clear?"

As Aaron was led out of the house barefoot, Sally attempted
to hug her terrified son, but Jaggar wouldn't release the boy's
arms. Wanting to appear resolute, trying not to cry, she took
his face in her hands and declared, "I love you. I don't want you

to be afraid. This is what's best." Then Jaggar hustled the boy outside, drove to the local airport, and flew Aaron to Escalante in a single-engine Cessna.

Over the next month, Sally called North Star several times a week to see how Aaron was progressing. The news was not encouraging. Her son, said North Star spokeswoman Daryl Bartholomew, was "belligerent and a whiner. All the other kids resented him." And the reports only became more negative as time went on. During a long phone conversation on March 30, Bartholomew informed Mrs. Bacon that Aaron's attitude was in fact so bad that it looked like he was going to have to repeat the program.

Jarid took Sally out to lunch that afternoon, during which he admonished her for sending Aaron to North Star. "You overreacted," Sally was scolded by her oldest son. "Aaron's problems aren't that serious. He doesn't belong at a place like that."

Twenty-four hours later, Aaron was dead. According to the autopsy, the cause of death was acute peritonitis resulting from a perforated ulcer. The contents of Aaron's gastrointestinal tract had leaked through two holes in his small intestine, spreading toxins and a massive infection throughout his abdominal cavity.

North Star explained that the ailment had surfaced without warning, so suddenly that heroic efforts by their staff in the field, a team of EMTs, and an emergency medical helicopter could do nothing to save Aaron's life. Preliminary reports from the Garfield County sheriff seemed to confirm North Star's contention that the tragedy was unavoidable, a freak accident.

Bob and Sally were shattered by the news. The last time they had seen or spoken with Aaron was the morning Jaggar had taken him forcibly from their home, frightened and bewildered. They had never had an opportunity to explain to their son why they were sending him to North Star. "After Aaron died," Sally says, "all I wanted was to get his body back.

I wanted to hold him and say good-bye. I wanted a chance to apologize."

When the body arrived at a Phoenix mortuary three days later, however, guilt gave way to anger. "As soon as I saw Aaron's face," Sally insists, "I knew something wasn't right." Pulling the sheet from the body, she was confronted with a visibly battered, extremely emaciated corpse. She started screaming hysterically and had to cover her eyes.

"His legs were like toothpicks," Sally reports, breaking into sobs. "His hip bones stuck way out, his ribs—he looked like a concentration-camp victim. There were bruises from the tip of his toes to the top of his head, open sores up and down the inside of his thighs. The only way we were even able to recognize him was a childhood scar above his right eye. The mortician told us he'd never seen a body in such bad shape."

"Right then it became obvious to us that Aaron's death was not an accident," says Bob Bacon. "We knew that something horrible had been done to him."

At the bottom of a ravine slicing into the parched uplands of central Arizona, an alligator lizard scurries up a boulder in the withering sun. A big, gawky sixteen-year-old—his cherubic face smudged with soot and bracketed by blond Botticelli curls—spies the reptile and plucks it from the rock with a lightning-quick lunge. "This is the tenth lizard I've caught," Craig announces proudly, clutching the quarry in his pudgy fingers. Then he slices off its head, pops it into his mouth, and gulps it down.

Craig is enrolled in a nine-week treatment program for troubled adolescents run by the Anasazi Foundation, a nonprofit corporation based in Mesa, Arizona. He is presently camped beside a rock-choked creek with three other wayward teens and their three college-age counselors. Some forty other

Anasazi students and their keepers are sprinkled among the adjacent canyons.

As Craig stokes the fire, Danny, fifteen, and Stuart, fourteen, hunker in the sand nearby, frowning in silence as they scribble in the journals they keep as part of their unorthodox treatment. Suddenly the quiet is broken by the deafening *whump-whump-whump* of a helicopter, which spirals down from the simmering sky to alight behind a nearby ridge. A terse radio conversation reveals that a student from another group, in the throes of methamphetamine withdrawal, is being evacuated to a distant hospital. As it turns out, the boy's condition isn't serious—he apparently faked a seizure to get out of the program—but in the wake of the "North Star incident" (as the counselors distastefully refer to it), the people who call the shots at Anasazi aren't taking any chances.

Sometime next winter, Lance Jaggar and seven other North Star employees, charged with felony child abuse and neglect in Aaron Bacon's death, will stand trial in Panguitch, Utah. Though Bacon wasn't the first teenager to die during wilderness therapy—nationwide, more than a dozen other deaths have occurred since such programs came into being in the seventies—the horror of his last days, detailed in a personal journal, has stirred up a hurricane of media attention. It has also generated unprecedented concern about the multimillion-dollar wilderness therapy industry.

The population of dysfunctional families and out-of-control adolescents is huge and growing. The demand for youth treatment far exceeds the capacity of available facilities. "There are a lot of desperate parents out there," muses Lewis Glenn, who oversees safety at Outward Bound USA, which has adapted a relatively small number of its courses for troubled adolescents and rejects the tough-love approach. "And many of them are looking for a quick fix: 'Here's my money; take my messed-up kid for a month and make him better.'"

Regardless of how the Bacon trial turns out, its long-term significance will rest on the crucial questions it has raised about wilderness therapy. Does it really work? How often? And at what risk? Who sees to it that the camps offer bona fide therapy and not just clumsy behavior modification?

As yet, none of these questions has been adequately answered. Nationwide, more than 120 companies are in the business of wilderness therapy, and a small but significant number of them—perhaps two dozen—employ harsh methods. By definition, treatment conducted miles from any road isn't easy to monitor. If the Bacon case is any indication, a flurry of vaunted regulations enacted five years ago by the state of Utah (in reaction to two other fatalities in Utah-based programs) accomplished little beyond giving the public a false sense of security.

Opinions about how society should respond range widely. In Panguitch—where North Star's attorneys will argue that Bacon was a faker whose genuine problems were ignored because he cried wolf too often—parents of other students in Bacon's group will maintain that North Star saved their kids from such evils as drug abuse, prostitution, and satanism, and should be allowed to resume business.

Others see the tragedy as a clear sign that tighter controls are warranted. "North Star's troubles have tainted the whole industry," laments Archie Buie, the founder of an organization called the National Association of Therapeutic Wilderness Camps. Comprising some thirty wilderness schools, the NATWC was formed in the wake of the Bacon fatality to establish accreditation standards and weed out dangerous operations.

Cathy Sutton, whose daughter Michelle died in 1990 at an inept wilderness school called Summit Quest, applauds the NATWC's intentions but remains skeptical that the industry can be policed from within. "There is too much money to be made by duping parents, abusing children, and risking lives," she declares bitterly. "There needs to be more government oversight." Sutton is using the $345,000 settlement she received from Summit Quest's insurer to establish a watchdog group of her own, the Michelle Sutton Foundation for Camp Safety.

Arguing that North Star is by no means the only program flirting with disaster, Sutton is particularly concerned about a New Mexico–based wilderness therapy camp called Pathfinders, run by a former Vietnam fighter-jet pilot named Michael Parr. Despite documented charges of abuse and an ongoing state investigation into its practices, Pathfinders continues to operate with impunity, at full capacity.

Doug Nelson—a professor of outdoor education at Brigham Young University who spearheaded the aforementioned licensing reforms in the state of Utah—argues that it isn't fair to tar the entire industry with the same brush. "All the bad press," he points out, "is the result of a few bad programs. When it's used right, the wilderness can be an incredibly powerful tool for helping troubled kids. We've found that you can do more in a month or two in the wild than you can in a year at a residential treatment center. Unfortunately, in the wrong hands, something that powerful can be very dangerous."

The belief that wilderness redeems the soul is as old as the Boy Scouts, as old as John Muir, as old as the Old Testament. But only in the last half-century has the concept of forging character on nature's anvil been packaged into a booming business.

In the early days of World War II, German U-boats began sinking great numbers of Allied merchant ships, forcing thousands of crewmen into lifeboats on the stormy North Atlantic. Surprisingly, the youngest, strongest sailors were often the first to die in the open boats. Disturbed by the fact that "the younger men seemed to lack self-reliance, confidence, and a compassionate bond with their fellow crew members that was so vitally essential to meet the challenge of a crisis," a German educator named Kurt Hahn decided to establish a school in Wales, christened Outward Bound, to rectify this deficiency.

After the war, Hahn's school expanded, offering the same arduous outdoors curriculum as a tool for molding Britons into higher achievers in peacetime society. In 1962, Outward Bound transplanted the program to the United States, opening a branch in the mountains of western Colorado. The standard twenty-six-day course included rock-climbing, bust-ass back-packing, and a three-day wilderness "solo."

Americans found the concept immensely appealing and signed up in swarms. Outward Bound opened additional schools from Maine to Oregon, and scores of OB imitators materialized to meet the unquenchable demand. By the 1970s, the nation was home to more than two hundred programs dedicated to self-improvement through outdoor adventure.

A disproportionate number of these OB-inspired programs originated in Provo, Utah, on the campus of Brigham Young University. The catalyst was an Idaho farm boy named Larry Dean Olsen, who enrolled at BYU in the mid-1960s. Olsen was a self-taught survival buff who knew a lot about chipping arrowpoints, making snares, and living off the land. To help pay his way through college, he started teaching evening classes in the rudiments of backcountry survival to local hunters and fishermen.

In 1968, the university asked Olsen to lead an experimental "expedition," based loosely on the OB model, for a group of students who were flunking out. The thirty-day course, held in the Utah desert, was a grueling physical trial. But most of the twenty-six kids who completed it showed a striking improvement in academic performance the following semester. It was promptly added to the standard undergraduate curriculum, proved to be hugely popular, and ultimately became a center-piece of the university's Department of Recreation Management and Youth Leadership.

Olsen—now in his fifties, a folksy, gregarious man with a fondness for buckskin clothing and didactic fireside yarns—went on to write a widely read book, *Outdoor Survival Skills*, which brought him minor celebrity. Although he was forced out of BYU in the early 1970s following allegations of misman-agement and sexual impropriety ("Larry liked the girls a little too much," explains one of his colleagues), the success and popularity of BYU's outdoor education curriculum continued to balloon after his departure.

BYU is closely affiliated with the Church of Jesus Christ of Latter-day Saints; the culture that spawned Larry Olsen's sur-vival courses and the programs that followed was profoundly shaped by Mormon values. As a consequence, the BYU wil-derness courses veered notably from the Outward Bound paradigm. The Mormon programs placed a greater emphasis on primitive skills—on living more directly off the land, on getting by without modern technology. And at their core was a spiritual component that had no equivalent in OB. The BYU courses were intended, first and foremost, to be deeply reli-gious experiences—to promote faith in the Mormon ideal and prepare young Saints for the coming of the Last Days.

With the evangelical zeal endemic to Mormondom, gradu-ates of the BYU courses established similar programs across the West. Most of these operated uneventfully, but there were serious setbacks that presaged what would happen to Aaron Bacon. In 1974, a twelve-year-old boy became dehydrated and died of heatstroke while enrolled in a program run by the Idaho Department of Health and Welfare. The next year, a young woman died while hiking across Utah's Burr Desert, also from dehydration, while participating in a course run by BYU. In each case, the staff was inexperienced, poorly trained, and inadequately equipped; both deaths would have been easily prevented with a few basic precautions.

"In those days," explains Larry Wells, a BYU alumnus who currently directs an exemplary program called Wilderness Conquest, "the staff at these programs received almost no training in things like logistics or safety. Often there'd be only one instructor for every thirty or forty students. Nobody had radios. People didn't carry enough canteens. Because we were doing 'God's work,' there was a strong belief that God would look after everybody."

The deaths in 1974 and 1975 served as a wake-up call. BYU hired Wells—who credits a BYU wilderness course with his own transformation from a seriously troubled youth to a responsible adult—to overhaul the program and establish adequate safety standards. But sending unruly juveniles into the wilderness is an inherently dangerous undertaking, and there continued to be accidents over the years that followed. In the mid-1980s, a thirteen-year-old boy fell from a cliff to his death while enrolled in a course run by the School of Urban and Wilderness Survival (SUWS), a commercial outfit with an otherwise spotless reputation. Another student contracted a fatal case of bubonic plague—he probably caught it from a squirrel—while attending another well-regarded commercial program, the Boulder Outdoor Survival School (BOSS). Vision Quest, a notorious wilderness program based in Tucson, Arizona, has racked up at least sixteen accidental deaths to date.

Most of the deaths cited above were noted by the news media, but no great hue and cry was raised, and wilderness treatment programs continued to proliferate through the 1980s. Like BOSS and SUWS, many of the new schools were launched by BYU alumni as privately owned, entrepreneurial ventures. By and large, however, none of the commercial programs made much money or attracted many students until a

brash, charismatic young man named Steve Cartisano burst
onto the scene in 1987. Applying the full brunt of his marketing genius, he quickly transformed a marginally solvent industry into a cash cow.

Stephen Anthony Cartisano was born to a Cherokee mother
and Italian-American father, from whom he inherited chiseled
features and piercing eyes. His childhood in Modesto, California, he has reported, was not happy: One parent was addicted
to heroin, the other beat him. Although Cartisano has been
known to interpret the facts loosely, he insists that the torment
he endured as a youngster gave him tremendous empathy for
troubled teens, and eventually motivated him to make a career
out of helping them.

Cartisano, who turned forty in August, joined the Air
Force in 1974 and was made an instructor at the prestigious
Fairchild Air Force Base Survival School—the school where
Scott O'Grady, the F-16 pilot shot down over Bosnia last June,
honed his survival skills. Eventually rising to the rank of staff
sergeant, Cartisano became a parajumper with the elite 129th
Aerospace Rescue and Recovery Group, and in 1979 was
awarded the Meritorious Service Medal for his role in a dangerous rescue in the Wasatch Range. While in the Air Force,
he became close friends with a Mormon airman and was bap-
tized into the LDS church. Soon thereafter, he moved to Utah
and enrolled at Brigham Young University.

Cartisano cut a dashing figure on campus. Eager to launch
a career in show business, he spent most of his time studying film and theater, and wrote a screenplay about the exploits
of a crack Air Force pararescue squad: the hero of his script
was a handsome, brooding parajumper of Mormon faith
and Italian-Cherokee descent named Steve Montana. Carti-

sano never made it to Hollywood, nor did he earn a degree from BYU, but while he was a student, he worked briefly as an instructor in one of the school's wilderness courses, and thereby found his calling.

After leaving academia, Cartisano took note of all the commercial wilderness programs being launched by BYU alumni and decided to start a school of his own. Toward that end he hired Doug Nelson—who had directed the BYU wilderness programs for many years and founded BOSS—as a consultant. "Steve told me he was going to charge nine thousand dollars for a two-month course," Nelson recalls. "At the time, most commercial programs were charging something like five hundred for a thirty-day experience, and I told Steve there was no way anyone was going to pay that kind of money."

Cartisano was undeterred. He christened his school the Challenger Foundation, advertised a course to be held in a remote corner of the Hawaiian Islands, and had little trouble finding parents willing to enroll their misbehaving offspring at nine bills a head. In January 1988, encouraged by this success, he moved Challenger to Utah and began running courses out of Escalante. He raised tuition to $12,500 and then $15,900, but the high cost did nothing to slow Challenger's exploding enrollment. By the end of the year, Cartisano had fifty employees on the payroll and had taken in more than $3 million in revenue.

Like Outward Bound, most Mormon-run wilderness schools were strongly influenced by the burgeoning human potential movement. The Mormon programs subjected their students to intense physical challenges, but the kids were generally treated with care and sensitivity, and a lot of attention was paid to their "feelings." Cartisano, coming from a gung-ho military background, disdained this softhearted, touchy-feely approach. Instead, he modeled his program on Vision

Quest—a hard-as-nails school that had been inspired by the movie *Billy Jack*—and ran Challenger with the in-your-face discipline of a boot camp.

"There was nothing complicated about the Challenger philosophy," Cartisano explains. "It was all about setting limits and sticking to them. Most of the kids we got were defiant, rebellious, and out of control. Every other type of treatment had failed for them. Many had been sent to us by the courts. We showed these kids that their actions had immediate consequences. The excuses they'd been using at home didn't cut it with Mother Nature. We taught them to be responsible, we took the hard edge off of them. And the results we got were phenomenal."

A videotape of a 1989 Challenger course shows a vanload of new students, looking shocked and confused, arriving at a remote desert location in the middle of the night to begin a sixty-three-day, five-hundred-mile forced march through the wilderness. A hulking bull of a man, wearing a bone necklace and an olive-drab biker-style bandanna, starts pounding on the van's windows and screaming at the kids to assemble around a bonfire. "Move it! Move it!" he bellows. "Get over to that fire *NOW*! . . . My name is Horsehair. For the next sixty-three days, you'll be under my care. . . . Do you understand!"

"Yes, sir!" the kids answer in unison.

"I can't hear you!"

"Yes, *SIR!*"

"I have a phrase that I use," Horsehair explains impassively to the camera. "I'm gonna love you till it hurts—you."

Horsehair—Cartisano's field director and chief lieutenant—was an Air Force vet with nine years' experience in military law enforcement. His legal name was Lance Paul Jaggar. He and another devout Mormon, Bill Henry—an Idaho acquaintance of Larry Olsen's who'd been active with the Explorer Scouts—supervised the day-to-day operations out of Escalante, allowing Cartisano to concentrate on sales and promotion from his Provo-area home—a lavish residence that had previously been owned by golfer Billy Casper.

A brilliant promoter, affable and articulate, Cartisano persuaded his "good friend" Oliver North to put in an appearance in Escalante at the height of his Iran-Contra notoriety, and alerted *The Salt Lake Tribune* to the visit. "It was just a couple of buddies getting together and me showing him my program," Cartisano demurred in print. "He might have wanted to get some ideas for his own dealings with troubled youth."

Cartisano hired a publicist who booked him on *Donahue, Sally Jessy Raphael, Geraldo*—"all the big talk shows," he boasts. "They loved me. For about a year, I was the darling of the media. I'd go on TV with kids who'd been through the program, these beautiful fourteen- and fifteen-year-old girls who'd talk about how they'd been out on the street stealing and doing drugs and turning tricks until Challenger changed their ways." It was an extremely effective pitch. Cartisano sealed the deal by guaranteeing that any Challenger alumnus who reverted to a life of delinquency could, for no additional charge, come back and repeat the course until he or she was straightened out.

"The television appearances were a marketing gold mine," says an ex-associate of Cartisano's. "Those talk shows are watched by precisely the audience Steve wanted to target. The phones were ringing off the hook. Parents begged him to take their kids. An incredible amount of money started rolling in. Unfortunately, Steve wasn't used to having money and didn't know how to handle it."

When Cartisano would go on the road to recruit customers, says the ex-associate, "sometimes he'd spend two thousand dollars a week to rent a Lamborghini. He'd run up thousand-dollar-a-night hotel bills. He'd drop ten or twenty thousand

bucks in a weekend wining and dining celebrities." Despite all
the money coming in, Challenger began having trouble paying
its bills. Checks bounced. Creditors started complaining. The
Internal Revenue Service inquired about $196,000 in unpaid
corporate taxes.

At the same time, charges started to fly that Challenger staff,
including Cartisano and two of his brothers, physically abused
their students. According to Max Jackson, the former sheriff of
Kane County (Challenger ran its courses in Kane and adjacent
Garfield County), "we pulled one kid from the program who
was so bruised and scarred he looked like he'd been at Ausch-
witz. When another kid tried to run away, Cartisano got in a
helicopter, found him, flew him up to the top of a mesa, and
slugged him in the gut a couple of times."

Although Cartisano was married and had four children,
Jackson alleges that "at one point he struck up a romance with
the mother of one of his students. He talked her into giving
him her Visa gold card with no credit limit. He ran up sixty-
five thousand dollars in charges before she realized she'd been
had. And at the same time Steve was sleeping with her and
taking her money, he was also carrying on a sexual relationship with the woman's thirteen-year-old daughter.

"Steve is real smooth, real slick," Jackson reflects. "He
likes to hear himself talk. But I'll tell you what: I went to the
FBI academy a couple years back, and in one of my classes
we studied the typology of sociopaths. Out of a list of twenty
characteristics, Steve was a perfect match with about nineteen
of 'em." By early 1990, Cartisano was embroiled in a number of
lawsuits filed by creditors and disgruntled clients, and the state
of Utah was investigating him on several fronts.

Cartisano dismisses his problems with the law as a personal
vendetta—Sheriff Jackson and the state, he insists, were "out to
get me. The charges were all based on allegations of messed-
up kids who were pathological liars and master manipulators

who would do anything to get out of the program. They knew that the fastest way to do that was to accuse the staff of abusing them." Defiant and unbowed, in 1989 Cartisano proclaimed, "There's no way on this earth I'll ever allow any petty bureaucrat to take over this program and turn it from a survival camp into a summer camp. They're going to find out they're messing with the wrong guy."

As Cartisano's financial and legal difficulties mounted, the Challenger admissions director—a woman named Gayle Palmer—quit to start her own wilderness therapy company, which she christened Summit Quest. Palmer had virtually no backcountry experience, and in fact knew little about either wilderness or therapy beyond what she'd gleaned from pitching Challenger courses to prospective clients. "But Palmer got tired of working for Steve," says Doug Nelson, "and decided she could run a program at least as well as he could, so she left Challenger, hung out her shingle, and went into business."

Five students were enrolled in the inaugural Summit Quest course, which cost $13,900 and was scheduled to last the canonical sixty-three days. Palmer sent the group to the arid Shivwits Plateau, near the North Rim of the Grand Canyon, under the supervision of two young counselors working for minimum wage. During the first several days, Michelle Sutton—a pretty, not particularly troubled fifteen-year-old who had enrolled voluntarily to regain self-esteem lost during a recent date rape—complained repeatedly of exhaustion, sunburn, and nausea. As the group hiked through the desert, she vomited up most of the water she tried to drink and pleaded that she could go no farther. The lead counselor—who had been instructed to ignore such protestations as manipulative behavior—told Sutton, "You have been sloughing off. You are now being warned."

On May 9, 1990, Sutton continued to complain of exhaustion and dizziness, and collapsed repeatedly during an ascent of 7,072-foot Mount Dellenbaugh. She begged for water, having consumed all of hers, but liquids were rationed and the other students were forbidden to share. Michelle's speech became slurred, she cried out that she couldn't see, and then she lost consciousness and died. Because the counselors didn't have a functioning radio, they weren't able to summon help until the following day.

Gayle Palmer insisted that Sutton had succumbed to a drug overdose, but the coroner found no drugs in her system and determined the cause of death to be dehydration. Cartisano was quick to lash out at Palmer in the media, accusing her of running a criminally incompetent program that besmirched the good reputation of the entire industry. "At Challenger," he gloated, "a tragedy like the one that killed Michelle Sutton could never happen."

Just six weeks later, it did. On June 27, 1990, four days after enrolling in Challenger, a sixteen-year-old Florida girl named Kristen Chase collapsed after completing a five-mile hike in near-100-degree heat. Once again, her counselors had thought she was faking it when she'd brought her problems to their attention. The counselors carried a radio, but instead of immediately calling for medical assistance when Chase went down, they tried to carry her to camp, and while they were doing so, her heart stopped beating.

The incident occurred south of Escalante on a high mesa called Fifty Mile Bench. During a previous emergency Cartisano had relied on the services of Classic Life Flight, a company that operated a fully equipped medical helicopter out of Page, Arizona. Classic could have flown to the site within twenty-five minutes, but Cartisano had been feuding with the company over an unpaid bill, so a tour helicopter from Bryce

Canyon was called instead; by the time it finally arrived, two hours had passed since Chase had stopped breathing. The coroner attributed the death, like that of Michelle Sutton, to hyperthermia and dehydration—the most basic and easily prevented hazard of desert travel.

Following Kristen Chase's death, the state of Utah charged Cartisano and his field director, Lance "Horsehair" Jaggar, with negligent homicide and nine counts of child abuse involving not only Chase, but other Challenger students as well. Jaggar, however, cut a deal with the Kane County prosecutor: he agreed to testify against Cartisano in return for having all charges against him dismissed.

The trial was held in Kanab, Utah, in September 1991. Jaggar and other Challenger employees testified under oath about beatings and other abusive treatment. "We had Cartisano on the ropes," says Sheriff Max Jackson. After five days of testimony, however, a mistrial was called when defense attorneys pointed out that the judge had forgotten to read the charges to the jury at the commencement of the proceedings.

The case was retried eight months later in the Salt Lake City area. "The second time around," says Jackson, "Cartisano knew what the prosecution's game plan was, and brought in a high-dollar attorney from New York. And then in the middle of everything, the prosecuting attorney started drinking real heavy and I had to arrest him for DUI. The upshot was, Cartisano was found not guilty. He got off scot-free."

Afterward, one of the jury members explained their verdict: "We weren't saying Cartisano was innocent, we were saying the prosecution didn't prove he was guilty. . . . We all felt like the program had some real problems."

Despite its failure to convict Cartisano, the state of Utah resolved to monitor the wilderness therapy industry much more closely. Many concerned individuals within the industry,

including Doug Nelson and Larry Wells, supported the crack-
down and came forward to help draft a set of strict regulations.
Prominent among the reformers pushing for the tough new
law were Lance Jaggar and Bill Henry, who zealously decried
the abuses of their former employer, Steve Cartisano.

Jaggar and Henry had earlier announced their intention
to start a wilderness therapy program of their own. They put
together the paperwork, submitted it to the appropriate agencies, and in October 1990, were granted a license to operate
in the state of Utah. Three months after the death of Kristen
Chase, the two individuals considered by many to bear most
of the responsibility for that tragedy were back in business.
They called their new enterprise North Star Expeditions.

"Of all the regions of the United States the Mormon Country
is the least known outside," observed the late Wallace Stegner.

> *For all the Chambers of Commerce which toot the scenic
> wonders of the red rock plateaus and mountain lakes, the
> Mormon Country remains comparatively untouched by
> the tourist traffic; the society which is actually more inter-
> esting than the country in which it was planted keeps to
> itself, aloof and as self-sufficient as Brigham could ever
> have hoped it to be.*

If Mormon society strikes outsiders as insular and hard
to fathom, it is particularly so in the small, isolated towns
that rise from the wind-scoured slickrock of southern Utah.
Escalante, in Garfield County, is one such community. In the
county seat of Panguitch, seventy miles to the west, where
Jaggar, Henry, and six North Star employees will be tried this
winter for the death of Aaron Bacon, a clerk in the sheriff's
office remarks, unbidden, "They're a different kind of people

over in Escalante. You ask me, everybody who lives there is weird."

Escalante (pronounced "es-ka-LANT" in the local patois) has had an influx of California retirees in recent years—the population has swelled to about eight hundred—and a new motel recently went up to siphon a few dollars from tourists passing through town on the national park circuit, yet the townsfolk merely tolerate these intruders—they don't welcome them. When Cartisano brought Challenger to Escalante in 1988, many of the locals were initially wary. But it was a good Mormon enterprise, and field director Lance Jaggar married a local girl—Barb Reynolds, from nearby Tropic. The company and its payroll provided a significant boost to the moribund local economy. Eventually the Challenger crew gained a measure of acceptance.

By the time Challenger, minus Cartisano, transmogrified into North Star (the name changed, but many of the personnel remained the same), the company had insinuated itself tightly into the civic fabric. When the state and the media started asking pointed questions about Aaron Bacon's death, most of the town rallied to North Star's defense. At the Circle D restaurant, a remark about Bacon prompts a curt warning from the waitress: "That's a real touchy subject around here. He was a drug addict, his parents was drug addicts, and now that he's dead, they want to blame somebody, so they're trying to wreck the lives of the folks who was trying to help him."

Aaron Bacon arrived in Escalante on March 1, 1994, in the custody of Lance and Barbara Jaggar. He was strip-searched, issued cheap boots and backpacking equipment, and then driven out into the desert to begin a ten-day acclimation process. Escalante lies 5,600 feet above sea level, and in March the weather there is harsh and wintry. As part of their treatment, students were required to keep journals, in which they were forbidden to use obscenities or "use the name of the

Lord in vain." The first backcountry entry in Bacon's journal reads:

> *I've been shaking from the cold since I got here. My body being used to the weather in Phoenix is going into shock. I feel like I'm going to die. . . . I am scared. I don't know when I can talk or if I can.*

Following the deaths of Michelle Sutton and Kristen Chase in 1990, the state of Utah enacted a codex of strict new regulations for the wilderness therapy industry. Under the new law, the weight of a student's backpack was not to exceed 30 percent of body weight. Each student was to have a sleeping bag, shelter, and ground pad whenever the temperature dropped below 40 degrees Fahrenheit, and a weekly change of clean clothing. Hiking was never to "exceed the physical capability of the weakest member of the group." Students were to receive a minimum of 1,800 calories of food per day. A single violation was grounds to suspend an operator's license.

Responsibility for enforcing the regulations, however, fell to a lone civil servant—a rotund, balding man named Ken Stettler, who was supposed to monitor more than a hundred youth treatment companies statewide. In fact, it was impossible for him to keep on top of that many programs, and North Star was among those that escaped close scrutiny. Stettler was a devout Mormon who knew Jaggar and Henry well and, as fellow Saints, trusted them implicitly—having been leading advocates of the tough new rules, he assumed they would abide by them.

(Stettler's confidence in Jaggar and Henry would remain steadfast even after Bacon's death. Immediately postmortem, he cleared North Star of any wrongdoing and allowed the program to keep operating—which it did for the next six months, until the Garfield County sheriff opened a criminal investigation in October 1994.)

But Jaggar and Henry made a mockery of Stettler's trust and brazenly flouted the regulations. Thirty-three students were enrolled at the time of Bacon's arrival, even though the school's land-use permit limited enrollment to twenty-six. Food was strictly rationed. Students were deprived of provisions, sleeping bags, and shelter as a matter of course.

Like Challenger, the North Star program was sixty-three days long and promised to take back misbehaving alumni at no additional charge. The counselors in the field were mostly twenty- and twenty-one-year-old high school graduates without formal training of any kind; the starting salary was $1,000 a month.

There was one credentialed therapist on the payroll—David "Doc Dave" Jensen, a clinical social worker—but Aaron saw him only once, on March 6. Following the Challenger model, therapy as it was dispensed by the North Star staff consisted almost exclusively of intimidation, deprivation, and paramilitary discipline. The program purported to build self-esteem, but only after the will of each student had been thoroughly and utterly broken.

Five days after arriving in Escalante, Bacon learned that one of his counselors had worked for Challenger. He noted in his journal that he'd once seen a television show about Challenger, and had heard that one of their students had died of a drug overdose. He didn't know that drugs played no part in the death of Kristen Chase, or that the tragedy had happened on the mesa that dominated the nearby skyline. Nor was he aware that Lance Jaggar, the man who now controlled his fate, had been charged with negligent homicide in the case.

Bacon was driven into town on March 7, where his shoulder-length hair was cut off and he was given a medical exam by a physician's assistant making a weekly visit from Panguitch (there is no doctor in Escalante, or even a resident PA). Bacon's weight at that time was 131 pounds. Blood and urine were taken to test for drugs. When the results came back, they indicated he had been using nothing but marijuana.

A day later, in a letter to his parents, Aaron wrote:

> *I'm trying to work this program as well as I can, but their philosophy about everything seems so different from anything that I've been taught. I can't believe you want me believing this stuff. . . . I've been told that "all therapists, counselors, psychologists, and psychiatrists are quacks." I've been lectured on the stupidity of believing in them. Last night around the fire my staff was talking about how useless AA, NA, CA, Alanon, and Alateen are. . . . I miss you mom, and you dad. . . . As I'm writing this and thinking about you all at home I can't help but cry.*

On March 11, the acclimation period ended, and Aaron's group of six students and two counselors headed into a labyrinth of spectacular sandstone defiles to commence a three-week backcountry trek. For the first two days, the students were deprived of food to "cleanse the toxins from their bodies." Aaron immediately suspected that he was physically incapable of performing much of what would be asked of him over the weeks to come. The weakest member of the party, he despaired of slowing everyone down and incurring the group's wrath. "I am scared of this program a lot right now," he recorded in his journal. "I've been sick all day with a horrible stomach ache."

Aaron got bad blisters on his feet, fell repeatedly, and had great difficulty picking himself off the ground wearing a forty-five-pound pack. Deep in an eerie, crepuscular defile called Little Death Hollow, he slipped and bashed his chin on the slickrock, inflicting a gruesome wound. "The staff don't seem to care one bit," he notes in his journal. "They were just mad because I broke a gallon [jug of water]. We get absolutely zero positive reinforcement. . . . If we do the smallest thing wrong we get reamed."

On March 15, he became too tired to carry his backpack, so he abandoned it. Because his pack held all his rations, he was forced to go without food until he retrieved the pack on the return trip two days later.

On March 18, while traversing the Gulch, a tributary canyon of the Escalante, the group had to wade through an icy, neck-deep pool that soaked all of Aaron's food and clothing. That night, shivering by the fire, Aaron wrote, "I'm so scared of everything: staff, slickrock, nights, the cold, my pack. . . . I'm getting blood everywhere, my nose has been bleeding for the past couple of days and even that scares me. I never got nose bleeds at home."

A day later, a counselor named Brent Brewer called Aaron aside and admonished him to work harder. Other counselors and students taunted him mercilessly for slowing down the group, and asked if he was homosexual. "Everyone seems like they are mad at me or don't like me for some reason," Aaron wrote, "and I think I'm pretty nice to them all."

On May 20, Brewer took Aaron's sleeping bag away as punishment for his bad attitude and replaced it with a thin blanket, despite the fact that nighttime temperatures dipped well below freezing. A day later Aaron wrote that he hadn't eaten in more than a day:

I feel like I am losing control of my body. I've peed my pants every night for the past three nights and today when we started our little hike I took a dump in my pants, I didn't even feel it coming, it just happened. . . . All the other students started to laugh. . . . I've been telling [the staff] that I'm sick for a while and they say I'm faking it. When they

talk to my parents they probably say that I'm a liar and I'm
faking everything.

It is unclear when Aaron developed the ulcer that ultimately killed him, but the stresses of the course had by now
severely exacerbated the ailment, and he was exhibiting clear
symptoms of physical distress. Yet nobody took his suffering
seriously. The next evening he wrote:

The cold and the wind is making me freeze up. . . . All I can
think about is cold and pain. Craig [Fisher, a counselor] is
back and he's so dagger mad like I've never seen him. . . .
I miss my family so much. My hands, my lips and face are
dead.

Aaron's journal ends with that entry, on March 21, but his
travails continued. Too exhausted to keep up with his group, he
abandoned his pack a second time as the students commenced
the grueling climb up Right Hand and Carcass Canyons to
the summit of the Kaiparowits Plateau. As a consequence, he
went without food, blanket, or sleeping bag from March 22 to
March 25 on the 7,000-foot mesa top, where nightly temperatures dropped below 22 degrees Fahrenheit.

On the twenty-fifth, Lance Jaggar and Bill Henry drove up
from Escalante and met Aaron's group on the Kaiparowits.
They gave him a blanket to replace his absent sleeping bag, but
took his cup away because "he wasn't keeping it clean." Jaggar also lectured him about malingering, and reiterated to the
counselors that Aaron was "a whiner and a faker" and should
be treated accordingly.

Bacon had been unable to control his bladder and bowels
for many days. After urinating all over himself during the
night of March 28, he was forced to hike without pants. The
group descended from the high country and retrieved Aaron's

pack, but Aaron was too weak to carry it. "The counselor got mad," recalls John Kulluk, one of the students, "and the rest of us had to carry it for him. Then, about a mile from camp, Aaron fell and couldn't get up so we had to carry him, too. While we were carrying him he puked all over Travis [another student] and talked about seeing purple stars, and a purple sky, like he was delirious."

Kulluk insists that when he first met Bacon "he looked normal," but by March 29 he resembled "a Jewish person in a concentration camp." That night Aaron complained once more of being seriously ill, says Kulluk, "but the staff just kind of blew him off and called him a faker. They yelled, 'Get off your lazy butt and go collect wood.' The next morning Craig [Fisher] got really mad, grabbed Aaron by the shirt, and pulled him to the latrine."

Three hundred miles south of where Aaron Bacon died, in a rock-strewn Arizona canyon, a teenage girl with unshaved legs, badly chipped nail polish, and a very dirty face kneels in the sand with a crude bow drill she's assembled from two sticks and a piece of twine. Concentrating fiercely, working the bow back and forth, back and forth, she twirls the spindle faster and faster against a block of cottonwood. Tendrils of smoke appear, and a moment later a tiny coal ignites, which she places in a pile of bark and coaxes into a blazing fire. "Nice fire, Angie!" proclaims Cheri, a similarly bedraggled waif who is kneading cornmeal and water into a wretched little pancake. "Too bad we don't have something better to cook on it than this crap."

Cheri, Angie, and another teen named Annie are seven weeks into a nine-week wilderness course run by the Anasazi Foundation. Like most of the kids who wind up in such programs, they were sent here for the typical adolescent transgressions: drinking, drugs, being sexually precocious, failing in school, shoplifting. "To get me here, my parents kidnapped me," Cheri, a petite sixteen-year-old from Boston, complains indignantly. "It was sick."

Having learned much about wilderness therapy in the abstract, I am sharing a camp with these young women and their three college-age counselors to understand how theory is put into practice here at Anasazi, which has a reputation for being one of the safest and most successful programs in the nation.

On the face of it there seems to be little difference between Anasazi and North Star. Both programs banish troubled teens to the wilderness with minimal equipment and meager rations in the hope of changing unhealthy, antisocial behaviors that more traditional forms of therapy have been powerless to alter. The kids learn how to sew clothing from animal skins, eat grubs and rattlesnakes, endure every sort of hardship the desert can dish out. But aside from these superficial similarities, Anasazi and North Star have little in common.

The night before, two boys from a nearby Anasazi group stuffed their sleeping bags full of clothes as a ruse, then stole away under the cover of darkness. Counselors discovered the escape half an hour later, picked up the kids' trail, and caught up to them shortly after dawn. At North Star, the strategy for dealing with such fugitives was to punish the little brats so severely that they'd think twice about trying it again. At Anasazi they took another approach.

"Where you guys headed?" the counselors calmly inquired of the runners. After suggesting that the kids return to the group, they added, "Of course, if you'd rather keep going in this direction, that's cool. We'll just tag along with you to make sure you're safe, okay?" The boys sheepishly confessed that they were tired and hungry and wanted to return to the group.

Anasazi's methods are rooted in the Mormon principle of

"agency"—that "God will force no man to heaven." According to this precept, righteous behavior cannot be induced through coercion. Nobody can *make* an unruly child straighten up and fly right; he or she must choose to do so.

"We don't lay many rules on these kids," explains Elizabeth Peterson, an irrepressibly upbeat twenty-year-old counselor. "They're not strip-searched when they arrive. If they insist on smuggling in contraband, they can—but we explain that they won't start making forward progress until they choose to turn over their drugs. The whole program is based on trust. It takes time and a lot of work to build that trust, but without it, there's really no point in even doing any of this."

This approach works at Anasazi because the young counselors are uncommonly sensitive, dedicated, and well trained—and because Anasazi turns away students who would not necessarily be disqualified from other programs: kids who exhibit assaultive or violent behavior, for example. If the kids here tend to be slightly more manageable than, say, the North Store clientele, plenty of them are deeply disturbed nevertheless, and their stay at Anasazi would never be confused with summer camp.

The kids are marched hard over rugged terrain. They sleep on rocky ground. When it rains, they improvise shelters from tree limbs and army ponchos or get wet. Once a week students are given a fifteen-pound food bag containing such staples as cornmeal, flour, and lentils—but no candy or junk food. The daily ration of 2,000 calories is extremely lean, and if a kid imprudently eats all her food early in the week, no more will be provided; she will have to subsist on wild plants, scorpions, or whatever else she can come up with until the next resupply. The Anasazi students with whom I spoke looked fit and healthy, but food seemed to monopolize most of their conversations and all of their fantasies.

Somehow, the Anasazi staff manages to impose discipline,

to get the kids to go along with the program, without resorting to threats. Seldom do they even raise their voices. Larry Dean Olsen, who established the Anasazi Foundation in 1988, shortly after Steve Cartisano launched Challenger, explains that intimidation is antithetical to the Anasazi philosophy. "That's Satan's tactic," he insists. "There's only two ways you can help a kid: love him and love him some more. You've got to guide him gently and prayerfully to the right path."

As Olsen's choice of words suggests, theological doctrine is an integral part of the Anasazi curriculum. Students and counselors sing hymns and recite prayers from the Book of Mormon several times a day. Ezekiel Sanchez, who cofounded Anasazi with Olsen, unabashedly describes the program as "a battle for kids' souls. The Book of Mormon makes it very clear: You're either on the Lord's team, or you're on Lucifer's team." The religious cant inevitably raises questions about the program's effectiveness in treating kids from outside the LDS community. But on the surface, at least, Anasazi appears to work wonders.

"For the first week, I couldn't stand being here," says Cheri as she warms her grimy hands by the fire. "I hated everything about Anasazi. But now I'm grateful that my parents made me come. This is the best thing that's ever happened to me. I've changed *so* much out here."

"It's true," Angie pipes in. "You should have seen Cheri when she first arrived. She cried all the time. She was mean to everybody. Now look at her: she's happy. The rest of us can actually stand to be around her. She's really changed. All three of us have."

After speaking candidly and at length with four groups of Anasazi students, out of earshot of their counselors, I am convinced that the program changed many of the kids in dramatic ways. But I am less convinced that the changes will stick.

A 1991 survey of Anasazi alumni found that 73 percent had

managed to stay away from drugs and alcohol a year after completing the program. Another study reported a 78 percent success rate in averting failure in school, 60 percent success with drugs, and 62 percent success at changing "oppositionally defiant behavior." These are respectable numbers, and anecdotal evidence offered by Anasazi is even more impressive. But as psychologists are quick to point out, the kind of self-reporting on which much of this evidence is based results in notoriously unreliable data.

No wilderness therapy program has ever been the subject of a scientifically rigorous, long-term study. When graduates of such programs return to the same environment that created their problems in the first place, there is little assurance that the kids won't revert to their old ways of acting out.

During a five-hour van ride with a batch of parents en route to be reunited with offspring after a sixty-three-day stint at Anasazi, I am vividly reminded that troubled kids are sometimes the product of seriously haywire families. After listening to one father—a self-important doctor from Kansas—pontificate smugly for much of that long ride, I wonder whether the child of this pathetic man would have been better served had Dad been shipped off to Anasazi instead of Junior.

And yet after I hear this father's story, culpable though he is, a part of my heart goes out to him—as it goes out to every parent in the vehicle as they recount their own doleful, distressingly familiar tales of children lost to drugs and petty crime and nihilistic adolescent rage. What would I do, I wonder uncomfortably, if I had a fourteen-year-old daughter who lived on the street and performed fellatio on strangers in order to buy crack cocaine—a child, say, who'd already been through every kind of conventional treatment available?

I am not Mormon, and the religious indoctrination I witnessed at Anasazi disturbed me. But even if I knew that the odds of solving my kid's problems were less than 50 percent—

even if they were less than 1 percent—I have little doubt that I would attempt to scrape together the money and hie my child off to Anasazi or someplace like it as fast as humanly possible. Given the alternative, what parent wouldn't?

Which underscores one of the biggest problems with wilderness therapy: too often parents are motivated to choose such treatment for their offspring by fear and guilt and unfiltered emotion—lousy criteria for making such a critical decision.

According to Mark Hesse, who has worked with adjudicated youths as director of the Santa Fe Mountain Center, "A bad program can do more than physically harm kids—it can do major psychological harm. Boot-camp-type programs are good at breaking kids down, but then what? When adolescents are hardened and desensitized, it's usually for a pretty good reason. Their screwed-up behaviors often serve as a useful kind of armor. It can be disastrous to take kids out into the woods, strip down their defenses, and then throw them back into the same snake pit that created them.

"You simply can't send a kid into the wilderness and expect miracles to happen, even in the best programs. The crux is what you do after the kid goes back home. For a wilderness experience to succeed, it has to be integrated with a comprehensive follow-up program that addresses all the kid's needs."

As the Anasazi van lurched down the rutted dirt road, the subject of Aaron Bacon came up. "I would never intentionally send my boy to an abusive outfit like North Star," offered one of the fathers, "but I realize that every program has risks."

"I guess there are some bad things that could happen out there in the desert," a mother rationalized. "But whatever my daughter is doing, I'm sure she's a whole lot safer at Anasazi than she would be in town, drinking and taking drugs with her friends."

This is what Sally Bacon believed about her son, too, of course, but she now warns that matters are not so simple. "I am not an unsophisticated person," she insists during a long conversation about the decision to send Aaron to North Star. "Bob and I were careful. We asked all the questions you're supposed to ask." She stares at her hands, and her eyes brim with tears. "Of all the treatment centers in America, why did I pick this one? How could I have been so wrong?"

"I think about what happened to Aaron every day," Mike Hill whispers in a voice thick with regret, more than a year after Bacon's death. A soft-spoken, baby-faced Apache raised by adoptive parents on the San Carlos Indian Reservation in Arizona, Hill will be a crucial witness for the state of Utah in the Bacon case. The defense will attempt to discredit Hill's testimony by attacking his character, pointing out that he has a history of drug abuse and that, as a counselor at North Star, he was investigated for having a sexual relationship with a seventeen-year-old male student. Hill says that none of these old allegations change what he saw and heard.

In September 1993, Hill was nineteen years old and "hanging out on the rez" when he and his best friend, Sonny Duncan, were offered employment at North Star. "There was no job interview or anything," Hill recalls. "I didn't really have any qualifications. They just hired us on the spot and drove us up to Utah. I thought it was going to be like a summer camp. I figured we would just chill out, spend a lot of time sitting around the campfire. Then we got there and learned different." Upon their arrival in Escalante, Hill and Duncan were rushed out to the field and, without training or supervision, left in charge of five students.

The North Star modus operandi was made clear to Hill right away. "My third day there," he says, "Horsehair [Lance Jaggar] came out and started yelling, shoving kids around, grabbing them in the crotch, poking them in the chest. He told one kid,

'Know what's gonna happen to you if you keep smoking pot? You're going to wind up in prison where big black bubbas like to fuck little white boys like you.'

"Horsehair almost never came out into the field except to beat up kids. One student, he kept cutting up his arms to try to get out of the program, so Horsehair wrapped him in a blue tarp, kind of like a burrito, and dragged him around on the ground. It freaked me out. These same people were trying to convert me to Mormonism, preaching about righteousness, and here they were doing this kind of stuff?"

Bacon wasn't in Hill's group, but they crossed paths now and then, and Hill liked the skinny, smart-ass kid from Phoenix. After not seeing Bacon for a couple of weeks, Hill encountered his group at the mouth of Right Hand Canyon on March 30, and was shocked at the boy's appearance. "He looked anorexic-like," Hill recalls, "with bones showing everywhere."

By this time Sonny Duncan, who was assigned to Aaron's group, had grown concerned enough about Bacon to radio the North Star office and request that Georgette Costigan—a staffer who was certified as an emergency medical technician— come out and look at him. She talked to Aaron for a few minutes, gave him a piece of cheese, and then drove back to town without checking any of his vital signs or performing a medical examination, satisfied that he was still faking his illness, despite the fact that he then weighed approximately 108 pounds, 27 pounds less than when he was "extracted" from his Phoenix home.

On March 31, because Aaron could no longer walk more than a dozen yards without collapsing, it was somehow decided that he should be taken into Escalante and start the course over again. Sonny Duncan radioed Mike Hill, who was camped nearby with a group of advanced students, and asked him to look after Aaron until a truck arrived to transfer the malingerer to town.

It was a cold, windy morning. At 10:30 A.M., when Hill walked over to Duncan's camp to take custody of Aaron, he found him sitting on a pit latrine. When he tried to stand, says Hill, "he started staggering like a drunk." As he did so, Duncan taunted and mocked Aaron, and insisted to Hill that Aaron had been starving himself because he wanted to die. Hill pulled up the boy's pants and started leading Aaron back to Hill's camp, but Aaron couldn't walk, so Hill instructed some of the students to carry him.

Back in Hill's camp, the counselor had Aaron lie down under a juniper out of the wind, and took two photographs of the emaciated youth. "Since you're trying to starve yourself," Hill admonished Aaron, "I'm going to show these pictures to your parents so they'll know what you're up to."

Aaron said he couldn't hear Hill, and that his vision had become a white blur. "I don't want to die, sir," he protested, and said that he had extreme pain in his lower abdomen.

Becoming increasingly alarmed, Hill got out the first-aid kit and tried to take Aaron's temperature—the first time anyone at North Star had thought to do so—but the thermometer was broken. Hill pulled a pouch of ocher-colored Apache "medicine" powder from a pouch in his pocket, sprinkled it around the sick youth, and told the other students to pray for Aaron.

A few minutes before two P.M., the voice of Eric Henry, one of Bill Henry's sons, crackled over the radio. En route to the camp in a North Star truck, Henry was calling to announce that he was almost there, and that Hill should "get the faker ready" to be transported back to Escalante.

According to Dr. Todd Grey, the forensic pathologist who headed the state's medical investigation of Bacon's death, at that time the contents of Aaron's stomach had probably been leaking through the perforations in his intestine for twenty-four hours or more. "He would have had low blood pressure, a fever, an elevated pulse rate, and exquisite tenderness of the abdomen," Grey says. "It would have been obvious that he was extremely sick. Any reasonable person, regardless of whether they had had any medical training, should have realized that Aaron Bacon was in need of immediate medical attention."

But when Eric Henry arrived that afternoon, North Star still had no intention of taking Bacon to a doctor; the boy was slated to join another group of new students and begin the course again. Unable to make it to the truck on his own, Aaron was picked up and placed in the backseat by Henry. Then for the next twenty minutes, he and the other counselors stood outside the vehicle chatting and making fun of Bacon.

At 2:54 P.M., the counselors heard Bacon banging his head repeatedly against the truck's rear window, so Hill went to check on him. The banging stopped. A minute later, Hill recalls, "I went to the passenger side of the truck to check again, and Aaron was just sitting there, staring off into space. His eyes were blank. I got really scared then. I checked his pulse and felt nothing."

They pulled Aaron from the truck, and Hill began performing CPR while Henry frantically radioed for medical assistance. "Everyone was freaking out," says Hill. "Someone kept screaming, 'Oh, shit! Oh, shit!'" Georgette Costigan arrived with her EMT kit in about thirty minutes, followed soon thereafter by the Escalante ambulance team and the Life Flight medical helicopter from Page, Arizona, but they were too late to do any good. Aaron was already dead.

When asked about the deaths at Challenger, North Star, and other programs, Steve Cartisano answers that because wilderness therapy saves the lives of so many children, an occasional fatality is a regrettable but justifiable cost of doing business. He calls it the "window of loss."

"Jaggar and Henry apparently share this view," muses Bob

Bacon as dusk falls over Phoenix, "and I find that despicable. Nobody from North Star has ever indicated to Sally or me that they are sorry for what they did to Aaron. They are not contrite in the least. Even now they seem convinced that they were performing a benefit to society. Their arrogance is incredible. And I don't think Jaggar and Henry are the only two people misguided enough to subscribe to this view.

"They call it 'tough love,' but I don't see that there was any love involved. It's all about using fear and humiliation and intimidation to break kids down. And we allowed these assholes to take our money and talk us into this 'extraction.' It's going to be very hard to forgive myself for that lapse of intelligence. But outfits like North Star prey on families in crisis. They lie to you. They tell you whatever you want to hear.

"Aaron was the only kid who died at North Star, but he wasn't the only one who was severely abused. I feel quite certain that many of the kids who survived the program have been scarred for life, emotionally and spiritually."

In the current political climate, many people view boot camps as a nostrum for the myriad ills afflicting the nation's youth. Paramilitary discipline is no panacea, however. It may be an effective tool for molding obedient soldiers and cohesive fighting units, but the available evidence suggests that intimidation is not the best way to instill such qualities as compassion, sound judgment, and self-respect. Brutality tends to become imprinted on the psyches of the brutalized, who thereby learn to regard savagery as acceptable behavior, and to treat others in the same inhumane fashion. Programs like North Star, it can be argued, do considerably more harm than good—both to the kids who attend them and to society at large.

Not all wilderness therapy programs are run like boot camps, to be sure. Larry Olsen's Anasazi Foundation, Larry Wells's Wilderness Conquest school, and the Aspen Achievement Academy, based in Loa, Utah, should not be confused with the likes of North Star, Pathfinders, or Challenger. But this remains an industry in which regulations are lax and the profit margins are extremely tantalizing. As long as the population of messed-up adolescents and desperate well-to-do parents continues to swell, wilderness therapy is likely to attract more than its share of shady operators and sociopaths.

A few months from now, Lance Jaggar, Bill Henry, Eric Henry, Sonny Duncan, Jeff Hohenstein, Craig Fisher, Brent Brewer, and Georgette Costigan will stand trial for felony child abuse and neglect. If convicted, each could go to prison for up to five years and face a $10,000 fine. If found not guilty, they will be free to return to the field of youth treatment.

Gayle Palmer, the founder of Summit Quest, was not charged with any crime following the death of Michelle Sutton. Although she was subsequently denied a license by the Utah Department of Human Services, Palmer brazenly resumed her operations in that state. In 1994, near Zion National Park, a scruffy, frightened fourteen-year-old girl wandered into a remote archaeological camp begging for help. It turned out that she was fleeing from a course Palmer had been running illegally out of St. George, the same town in southern Utah from which she had operated Summit Quest.

In the years since Steve Cartisano was acquitted of criminal charges stemming from the death of Kristen Chase, he has directed wilderness programs in a succession of Caribbean locales, sometimes under the alias Scott Richards, generating allegations of abuse and fraud wherever he has landed. In 1993, police in San Juan, Puerto Rico, discovered five boys hog-tied in a car with nooses around their necks; their keeper explained that the kids were enrolled in one of Cartisano's courses and had been bound to keep them from escaping.

Because Cartisano is being investigated for insurance fraud and other swindles, and owes a lot of money to a lot of people (he even stiffed Charles Brofman, the New York attorney who got him off the hook for Chase's death, for tens of thousands of dollars in legal fees), his precise whereabouts are a sensitive matter that he prefers not to divulge. During a recent phone conversation, however, he can't resist mentioning that he's back in business, "running pretty much the same kind of program I've always run." At last report, he had raised tuition to $20,000 and was finding no lack of customers.

Unrepentant, Cartisano explains that his past problems were "blown way of proportion by the tabloid media." There are still plenty of parents who applaud his hardheaded brand of treatment, he insists, and are grateful to him for straightening out their offspring. "Our clients come from all over the United States," he says of his current program, based in Costa Rica, the name of which he declines to reveal. "I take kids sailing. We don't have to put up with any ridiculous regulations or inspections down here. Things are going really well."

A CLEAN, WELL-LIGHTED PLACE

It is the kind of blustery March morning that feels about ten degrees colder than it actually is. A light drizzle is falling. The wind, sweeping in from across Puget Sound, turns the sea off Washington's Whidbey Island the color of lead. Christopher Alexander, iconoclastic architect of international repute, author of what some consider the most important ideas in architecture of the last century, is perched on a tree stump on a wooded hilltop, pondering the layout of a house that is to be built there. Yellow tape has been strung between poles stuck into the ground to form a rough three-dimensional outline of the structure-to-be, and he is staring at this flimsy skeleton intently, trying to figure out where the kitchen doorway should be located.

Alexander is a large-framed man, with a workingman's broad hands and the face of a good-natured cherub; dressed as he is in a rumpled yellow shirt, stained corduroys, and a jacket lined with polyester fleece, he looks more like a cabdriver, say, or a hot-dog vendor than someone accustomed to the rarified aesthetic atmosphere of architecture's loftiest reaches. In fact, Alexander considers himself no mere architect, but the modern equivalent of a master builder who is reintegrating the functions of architect and builder that, in his opinion, have become dangerously segregated in the present day.

Other architects would determine the location of the kitchen doorway by sitting down at a drafting table with a pencil and paper. Alexander believes that to make a building right you must do a large part of the designing at the construction site itself, working out the details and continually modifying the design as the building is erected. He creates a building in the manner of a sculptor shaping a piece of clay: add something here, stand back and assess the effect, take a little off over there, keep fine-tuning the elements until the form feels just right. Guiding him is a body of generic—and generative— design rules he's derived from building forms over the ages.

For this particular project—a two-story house of eleven or twelve rooms and about three thousand square feet, planned for clients who will both work and reside here—Alexander and one of his associates first spent a few days just sitting at the site, trying to determine what physical configuration would make it come to life. The little clearing at the top of the island knoll, rising as if from a sacred grove, was the obvious spot; but after spending some time there, Alexander says he realized that the clearing had to be preserved intact, with the building curling around it at the edge of the forest itself. Later, with the building's basic volume and placement in mind, Alexander spent a week on the site with his clients, staking out the building and brainstorming about its interior. At one point, when the exact configuration of kitchen, living room, and dining room was at an impasse, Alexander asked his clients to close their eyes and describe exactly what they could see upon entering the house; "very clearly and beautifully," he says, the husband began to describe "a long, endless chain down to a particular spot in the forest, with the rooms like beads on a necklace."

That's the feel it will have, enhanced by the "patterns" that Alexander feels are universal, as well as by some unusual construction techniques of his own. The master bedroom will have an eastern exposure—because for centuries the gradually building light of sunrise has been the most natural and comfortable way to wake. Although the house will be sixty feet long, it will be only about sixteen or seventeen feet wide, partly because of the site, but also because the longer and narrower a building is the more beautiful the light that suffuses it. On principle, there will be light entering from two sides of every room. Ceiling heights will be varied. And the accoutrements that personalize an interior—the window seats and benches, the alcoves, shelving, and such—will be added not as final touches but will be part of the structure from the beginning, so that the building evolves as much from the inside out as vice versa. "Like a cocoon," Alexander says. All through the process, as the building progresses and changes, Alexander will be working not from detailed blueprints, but from sketches and full-scale mock-ups of critical parts of the structure, made out of cardboard, scrap lumber, tree limbs, pieces of string.

Alexander's methods are not only unusual; they are seditious. He believes that the architecture-construction establishment is riddled with conceptual dry rot, that it should be razed and completely rebuilt. For the past fifty years, he declares flatly, "architects have been screwing up the world." His colleagues, he says, have abandoned what should be at the core of all architecture—the creation of buildings that not only provide shelter but strike a soothing chord deep in the psyche—in favor of "concept-ridden structures that seize your mind, but which lack feeling altogether."

Of course, Alexander is not alone in his dislike of the austere boxes of glass, steel, and concrete that have been springing up across the land since the '30s, when Ludwig Mies van der Rohe's aphorism "less is more" was embraced as unassailable architectural scripture. But most other critics of what has come to be known as Modern architecture—the so-called Postmodernists, the Whites, the Los Angeles Silvers—believe that there is nothing wrong with the state of architecture that can't be set right with a few innovative strokes of a mechanical pencil, backed up with some fancy new language. The glass boxes can be given curved walls, perhaps, or "historically evocative ornamentation," or striking colors, or "highly articulated" shapes; they can be adorned with "ironic references" to classical architectural forms. Alexander, however, regards such efforts as cosmetic tinkering that in no way addresses what's really wrong with our buildings. Crowning an imposing 648-foot granite skyscraper like Manhattan's AT&T Building with a pediment the shape of a gargantuan Chippendale highboy might be a wry architectural statement when the building is viewed from afar, he argues, but it does not fundamentally alter the fact that, for those who must spend their days inside it, the building is still an imposing 648-foot box.

For Alexander, the answer does not lie in ever more clever shapes contrived at the drafting table or in new architectural fashions. "What we are really talking about is changing the processes by which buildings are made—not the 'things' but the processes by which they are conceived and funded and regulated and constructed." What is required, he believes, is nothing less than "a shattering revision of our attitude to architecture and planning."

Alexander has dedicated much of the past quarter century to formulating the precise form that these shattering revisions should take. His conclusions have been set forth in a body of work published by the Oxford University Press: *The Oregon Experiment* (1975), *A Pattern Language* (1977), *The Timeless Way of Building* (1979), *The Linz Café* (1982), and *The Production of Houses*, released this year. These books have won Alexander a following both within his profession and outside it. His ideas are well represented in the curriculum at three important United States architecture schools—the University of Southern California, the University of California at Berkeley, and the University of Oregon—and there are bastions of young Alexander disciples in such cities as Bern, Tokyo, and Hannover, West Germany. He and his associates at the Center for Environmental Structure, the think tank/architectural firm/construction company that Alexander founded in Berkeley in 1967, have applied the ideas to more than sixty projects since the early '70s. Largest among them is a $10 million campus just built for the Eishin Gakuen, a university-affiliated high school outside Tokyo.

Among his prominent supporters is Sim Van der Ryn, a former California state architect who has designed work for intentional communities such as Findhorn in Scotland; he calls the ideas in Alexander's book *A Pattern Language* "the most important contribution to thinking in design and architecture in this century."

But Alexander's messianic tone and utterly uncompromising stance have rankled not a few in his profession. For Alexander, understand, does not say his methods are *one* way to create good buildings; he insists, without equivocation, that "there is no other way in which a building or town which lives can possibly be made."

At the core of Alexander's philosophy is the belief that architecture must not be approached as an abstract art form, but as a powerful social instrument—indeed, as the very framework of society. It is the architect's duty, therefore, to create unselfconsciously beautiful structures that bring harmony and order to the world. That not all architects share his ideas about the role of architecture or his definition of beauty—and some intentionally erect disharmonious structures on the landscape—makes Alexander "incredibly angry." "I find that incomprehensible," he says. "I find it irresponsible. I find it nutty."

Peter Eisenman is an influential New York architect whose ideas about architecture run 180 degrees counter to Alexander's. He designs extremely abstract buildings that have been called "explorations into pure form"—stark, complex structures that are intentionally "incongruent" and "antihumanist" to reflect the charged anxiety of the nuclear age. In 1983, in the course of a public debate at Harvard, Alexander told Eisenman, "People who believe as you do are really fucking up the whole profession of architecture right now, by propagating these beliefs."

Alexander feels strongly that real, honest-to-god beauty in a building—the kind of architecture that speaks to the soul—is not some slippery value that changes according to personal preference or the ebb and flow of fashion, but is a hard-and-fast thing. "The fact is," Alexander says, "that the difference between a good building and a bad building, between a good town and a bad town, is an objective matter. It is the difference between health and sickness, wholeness and dividedness, self-maintenance and self-destruction."

Good buildings, Alexander believes, "are alive." They have a "timeless quality, a sleepy awkward grace." When asked to cite examples, Alexander will mention Gothic churches, the old farmhouses of Norway and Colonial New England, the hill villages of the European Alps, the mud huts of Central Africa, the temples of Japan.

Not coincidentally, architects had little or nothing to do with the creation of the centuries-old structures Alexander admires so much. Those buildings were shaped by masons and carpenters according to a repertoire of details that had been worked out, refined, and passed along over the course of many generations as a way to solve recurring design problems. Alexander calls these repeatedly used solutions "patterns"; a collection of individual patterns large enough to create entire buildings and towns becomes a "pattern language."

In a village in the Swiss Alps, for example, the solution to the design problem, What should the top of a building look like? might be a pattern consisting of a steeply pitched roof with large eaves, which would serve to protect the house from large accumulations of snow and heavy mountain rains. Over the ages, the theory goes, such a pattern becomes rooted in the psyche in an almost archetypal way, so that an Alpine house without large eaves ends up failing not only on a practical level, but it just doesn't *feel* right either.

Although present-day architecture also is created by pattern languages, according to Alexander, those of this century have broken down. The language of the Modern movement, for example, is an amalgamation of patterns such as flat roofs without eaves; no colors except for white, beige, gray, and black; no decoration. These patterns have become so contrived and artificial, "so brutal, and so fragmented, that most people no longer have any language to speak of at all—and what they do have is not based on human or natural considerations."

To right what's wrong with our architecture, Alexander believes we should simply ignore all the clever new ideas of our architects—if not do away with the profession altogether—and go back to building from a simple, sensible pattern language based on a timeless, universally shared aesthetic. By 1977 Alexander had painstakingly compiled just such an animal, described in great detail in his book *A Pattern Language*.

A Pattern Language is a remarkable book that seeks not merely to explain good designs, but to *generate* them—it is a sort of architectural cookbook intended to demystify the design process and allow any layperson or group of persons to design any part of the environment for themselves. It applies equally to the design of houses, public buildings, neighborhoods, streets, gardens, individual window seats. The book consists of 253 patterns, each outlining "a problem which occurs over and over again in our environment, and then describes the core of the solution to that problem in such a way that you can use this solution a million times over without ever doing it the same way twice."

The book covers everything from the layout of entire cities to the "correct" dimensions for the trim boards that surround window openings. It is organized so that each pattern leads logically to the next, guiding ordinary folk through the design process step-by-step. A sampler of what is advocated: communities and towns should be designed and built in a piecemeal, organic fashion rather than by sweeping "master plans" and massive projects; buildings should be no higher than four stories; no more than 9 percent of the land should be devoted to parking spaces; buildings should be long and thin, with the most important rooms placed along the south side and the rooms in which people sleep placed to the east; every room should have access to natural light on at least two sides; common rooms should have intimate alcoves placed at their edges; ceiling heights should be varied throughout a building; windows should be made of many small panes instead of large sheets of plate glass (if there is a beautiful view, it shouldn't be spoiled by large windows that gape incessantly at it).

However, these patterns are not just a reflection of one man's architectural taste: Alexander arrived at them after more than eight years of objective experimentation and study, conducted both at Harvard's Center for Cognitive Studies and at his Center for Environmental Structure. Thus, each pattern, Alexander argues, may be looked upon as scientific hypothesis: all are tentative and free to evolve with new experience and observation. But he is confident that "many of the patterns here are archetypal—so deeply rooted in the nature of things that it seems likely they will be a part of human nature and human action as much in five hundred years as they are today."

According to Stephen Grabow, an architectural scholar from the University of Kansas who has written a biography of Alexander, architectural history records few, if any, instances of architects treating the question of design as a scientific problem. However, the strong empirical slant of *A Pattern Language*—Alexander's contention that good designs come from a set of objective rules and not the creative brilliance of individual designers—created quite a stir in architectural circles, no doubt partly because it poses a threat to business as usual. Perhaps the most often heard criticism of the book is that its 253 specific rules will produce buildings that look monotonously similar. To this, Alexander replies, "You could say the same thing about the human genetic code or the grammatical rules that operate on a language."

There are those who might refer to Alexander's ideas in a not entirely kind way as being quintessentially Californian. Alexander has in fact lived in Berkeley since 1963, but most of the twenty-six years of his life before that were spent in Europe, and his thinking probably reflects the values of the Old World as much as it reflects the New World ideals of California.

Born in Vienna in 1936, Alexander was the only child of two classical archaeologists. As a child, he was something of a prodigy in math and science; he won top scholarships first to Oundle, the prestigious, science-oriented British prep school, then to Cambridge University. In 1953, shortly before embarking on his university studies, he happened to see an exhibit of architectural photographs that excited him so much that he decided then and there to become an architect. At the urging of his father, who was "horrified" at that prospect, Alexander studied math as an undergraduate, but after taking his degree, he entered the university's architecture school.

His experience there was frustrating in the extreme. To Alexander's scientifically inclined mind, in order to carry on any sort of intelligent discourse about architecture one first had to be able to evaluate it in an objective way. He wanted to get right to the nub of "what made things beautiful" but found that nobody seemed interested in exploring matters at that murky depth. So after two years he departed for the United States to continue his dogged pursuit of the essence of architectural beauty at Harvard. His doctoral thesis there is a now well-known work titled "Notes on the Synthesis of Form," an attempt to empirically determine exactly what was going on in a good building design. Pointedly, the examples of good design he chose to illustrate his thesis were not drawn from the creations of the hottest architects of the day—Mies van der Rohe, Charles-Édouard Le Corbusier, Walter Gropius, or even Frank Lloyd Wright—but from the traditional structures of preindustrial societies.

After Harvard, Alexander went to India for a year to take a firsthand look at preindustrial architecture and the forces that shape it. He built his first building there, a small school, and then in 1963 returned to the United States to take a teaching position with the architecture school at the University of California at Berkeley, a job he still holds today.

Presently, Alexander is best known as an architectural theorist, as a thinker rather than a doer. This, he has said, "makes me immensely sad, because it is so far from the truth and because my heart is so much in the actual task of building." Although Alexander does indeed spend many hours not taken up by teaching in a dark and cluttered basement office, hunched over a Radio Shack computer turning his ideas into words, he does turn those ideas into buildings. It is as a licensed general contractor that he, along with his crew at the Center for Environmental Structure, has created his sixty-plus buildings—among them the center's own new offices in Martinez, California.

The construction-based line of criticism against Alexander's "timeless way of building" is that designing a structure on site while it is being built is much less efficient—and inevitably more expensive—than giving a construction crew a detailed, finished set of blueprints and telling them to go at it. Alexander denies this. By eliminating much of the drafting work that goes into the blueprints, he argues, he is able to devote more time, and allocate more money, to the construction process itself.

Alexander's claim that he can design buildings that are both superior to and competitively priced with conventionally produced buildings is supported by a low-cost housing project in Mexicali, Mexico, that he designed and built in 1975 along with a group of Berkeley students and the families who were to live in the houses. Each of the thirty houses were built for about $3,500, approximately half the cost of comparable buildings in Mexico at the time. According to the architecture critic Martin Filler, "The results at Mexicali are extremely simple in appearance, but have a special quality rarely present in housing for the poor. . . . These houses have been made with real concern for how good these rooms will be to live in and how they will nurture a sense of individuality, family, and community."

Alexander tries to keep costs down by cutting corners in materials and labor wherever appearance or quality is not crucial and by coming up with some very innovative construction techniques. He devises new ways of building, he says, by "deliberately putting myself out on a limb so that the pressure of having to get off that limb forces a solution." This also means that Alexander's clients have to place a great deal of trust in him.

Alexander's way of building does away with a valuable system of checks and balances that exists in the conventional building process: in the typical balance of power between architect and contractor, the architect makes sure the contractor doesn't try to pull any fast ones, and the contractor keeps an eye out for potential weak points—a roof design, say, that is likely to develop leaks over time—in the architect's plans.

A few years ago the American Institute of Architects forbade its members from becoming general contractors, believing that to wear both hats on the same project constituted a serious conflict of interest. Yet it is one of the most basic tenets of Alexander's methodology that the architect *must* wear both hats, that the benefits of having the architect serve as the builder outweigh the risk that the client will be taken advantage of.

In 1982 Alexander and his associate Gary Black designed and built a home in Albany, California, for a young couple named André and Anna Sala and their two children. Anna confirms that "one of the things about Chris is that you have a certain amount of blind faith, and that is very difficult. You're trusting him with your life fortune, with all your dreams." In fact, the Salas' home, when it was finished, surpassed their expectations. By almost any measure the house possesses rare beauty. "Building this house," says André, "is the single most important thing I've done in my life."

Not all of Alexander's endeavors have turned out so happily, however. Alexander has designed buildings only to have the projects called off at the last minute when clients got cold feet about his unusual methods. That, Alexander believes, is to be expected. "When, in the early stages of a project, the thing starts to have qualities that aren't exactly like what people are used to from working with conventional architects and contractors, it is easy for them to freak out," he says. His most dissatisfied client, Alexander openly volunteers, is a developer named Richard Erganian.

Impressed by Alexander's ideas about sensitive, human-scale building, Erganian initially hired him to build the first structure of a planned $400,000 shopping plaza in Fresno, California: a giant redwood trellis to shade an open-air farmers' market. Erganian paid the Center for Environmental Structure more than $4,000 in design and engineering fees, and another $42,500 to erect the trellis—only to begin souring on Alexander, he says, because of the "loose ends" he felt the architect left him to take care of and because a concrete floor, which cost an additional $12,000, was not finished to the standards he had expected.

Alexander says he had cautioned Erganian beforehand that

"we are going to build you a very beautiful building for the price of a bland, unremarkable two-by-four construction, but you have to realize that in order to do it, you have to give up certain things. Some things are going to be finished a little bit rougher than if your average Fresno contractor had done them."

Cosmetic imperfections aside, the trellis is a handsome structure—a fact that Erganian acknowledges. And Alexander went on to design the rest of the shopping plaza. Concerned that any loose ends that might develop on this much larger project could prove prohibitively expensive, however, Erganian showed Alexander's preliminary plans to a contractor he had worked with before, to corroborate Alexander's estimates—only to find that it was impossible for a conventional contractor even to submit a bid from the sketchy plans that are part of Alexander's unorthodox design methods. When Alexander wanted to begin construction before his plans were complete enough to receive the building department's final approval, Erganian says, he began to "put the skids on" as a client. Alexander has yet to finish the plans and secure a building permit, according to Erganian; Alexander says he is unwilling to go on until he has a building contract for the project from the developer. As things stand now, it seems doubtful that the shopping center—plans for which have cost Erganian, all told, close to $50,000—will ever be built, although Alexander says he is still hoping to reestablish their relationship.

Alexander insists that if Erganian had only been able to suspend his doubts, the project would have turned out beautifully. That has indeed been the case with Alexander's most impressive accomplishment to date, the Eishin Gakuen campus. The first thirty buildings of the $10 million project were completed within 10 percent of budget and on a very tight schedule, and show impeccable workmanship (thanks, in no small part, to the skill of Japanese craftspeople). But successful though it was, this project, too, had its rocky moments. Apparently Alexander's methods were so confounding and threatening to standard practices that midway through the job, one of the Japanese construction companies involved in the project offered the client $80,000 in cash if he would fire Alexander. The manager of the school, Hisae Hosoi, turned down the money, kept Alexander on, and reports that the faculty and students are currently "very happy every day" with their new campus.

The title Alexander has given to the book he is writing about the creation of the Eishin Gakuen is *The Battle for the Life and Beauty of the Earth: A Struggle Between Two World-Systems.* For Alexander, it seems, getting his ideas accepted has always been something of a battle, and he expects that will continue to be the case for some time to come. But, he says with customary assurance, "I am quite certain that by the end of this century and in the next, when these facts about buildings are no longer considered to be idiosyncrasies of any one person's theory but are indeed understood as the most fundamental facts about space, then all buildings will once more take their place in the three-thousand-year-old class of buildings that make sense. And at that point in the future," he goes on, "the peculiar shape of mid-twentieth-century buildings will in retrospect be seen for what it was—a temporary distortion, caused by willful refusal to grasp facts which are timeless."

FRED BECKEY IS STILL ON THE LOOSE

For longer than I've been climbing, for longer than I've been alive, the most talked-about piece of writing in the sprawling literature of mountaineering has been a mysterious tome known as the Little Black Book. Only a single copy is said to exist. Between its well-thumbed covers is a top secret, continually updated catalogue of the planet's finest unclimbed mountaineering routes: the highest, steepest, most extravagantly sculpted chunks of vertical ground that have yet to be groped by chalk-smeared human hands. The author of this fabled work is a resident of the Pacific Northwest, name of Wolfgang Friedrich Beckey—although folks are careful to address him as Fred, or just plain Beckey, or practically anything except his given name, lest they feel the sting of his unholy wrath.

Some say that Beckey's Little Black Book is apocryphal, that it's merely the product of too much wine and too much idle talk around too many campfires. "Oh, no," counters Sybil Goman, a free-spirited forty-two-year-old glaciologist who is the most recent in a long, turbulent string of Beckey's female companions. "There really is a Black Book. I've seen it. It's crammed full of notes about unclimbed peaks, big north faces that were overlooked by the mapmakers, last great problems in out-of-the-way corners of obscure ranges, that sort of thing. Fred guards it with his life."

The intense secrecy is understandable, because climbing where no one has ever climbed before *is* Fred Beckey's life,

PUBLISHED IN *OUTSIDE*, JULY 1992

and has been for more than half a century. His affairs have orbited so tightly around the hot sun of cutting-edge climbing that virtually everything else was long ago scorched from his existence. Beckey, understand, is the original climbing bum. Nowadays, of course, every crag from Smith Rock to the New River Gorge is crawling with pierced-eared rock rats who've copped an attitude, hit the road, and are living in tents in the dirt. But most of them are just temporarily slumming; within a few years, they'll be back in suburbia attending PTA meetings.

For Beckey, climbing is no mere pose. Back in the 1930s, he stripped his life of everything that might impede his campaign on the heights, and five decades later the mountains are still all that matters. The closest thing he has to a home is a secondhand Volkswagen with 400,000 miles on it. From the erudite tone of the seven mountaineering books he's authored, one would never guess they were scribbled in Burger Kings on the backs of place mats pilfered by the stack from the front counter. He has duffels of battered climbing hardware cached in the basements of acquaintances across the West, but the rest of Beckey's possessions wouldn't crowd a small closet.

Thanks to his single-minded focus, Beckey has achieved a kind of quirky, enduring magnificence to which attention must be paid. He is the Pete Rose of mountaineering, an alpine Charlie Hustle, climbing's foremost collector of big league hits, the most prolific first-ascensionist in the 206-year history of the sport. He has shared a rope with many of the premier climbers of the age—Yvon Chouinard, Layton Kor, Fritz Wiessner, Royal Robbins, Heinrich Harrer—and his creations include a disproportionate number of the most remarkable climbs in North America. Nobody, not even Beckey, knows precisely how many virgin lines he's plucked over the decades, but the tally must be close to a thousand. Greatness, however, hasn't come cheap. And the tab for Beckey's formidable obsession might finally be coming due, at the age of sixty-nine.

It's four A.M. on a winter morning. A caustic wind rattles the walls of the tent, which is pitched high in the snowbound North Cascades. "Jesus Christ, you see a bottle of Nuprin over there, any Nuprin?" demands Beckey in the fractured, elliptical mutter that characterizes Fredspeak. "Thought I brought a bottle of Nuprin. Jesus Christ. A little white bottle, plastic, I don't know, Nuprin. Maybe I forgot it, I don't know. You got any aspirin on you? Some aspirin? Jesus Christ."

By the time the sun has risen above the serrated eastern skyline, Beckey, Mark Bebie—a frequent ropemate of Fred's—and I are out of the tent, bundled against the cold, and starting to climb. Beckey, who is quick to confess that he "isn't a morning person," is not a pretty sight. As one of his ex-girlfriends warned me, "Fred in the morning is a bundle of aches and wrinkles with legs. It hurts to see him move." His face is a gaunt, astonishing matrix of furrows etched deep into leathery flesh, framed by wisps of shoulder-length hair whipping crazily in the wind. It's apparent that his hunched-over frame is stiff and creaky, but his sinewy arms and oversize hands hint at untapped reserves of power, and Beckey chugs up the slopes of Sahale Peak at a steady clip that, however painful, enables him to hold his own with climbers half his age. Which is fortunate, because that's how old almost all of Beckey's partners are these days.

Today Beckey's morning disposition is even more toxic than usual, owing to an unexpected change in plans. When he recruited Bebie and me for this three-day expedition, it was to make the first winter ascent of a mountain that Beckey had long had his sights on, a project considerably more ambitious than Sahale, the 8,680-foot peak that we are presently climbing. Last night, after arriving at our campsite, Bebie and I decided the original goal was too distant to be practical, and consequently staged a mutiny, proposing Sahale—an easy but handsome spire rising directly above our tent—as an alternative.

After more than an hour of heated argument, Bebie and I prevailed. Fred has been holding it against us ever since. "I don't know why you guys even came on this trip," he sputters, "if you didn't want to climb something worthwhile. Something worth climbing, Jesus Christ, I don't know. I did Sahale thirty years ago with a *girl*, and she'd never even climbed before, Jesus Christ."

By noon, however, when we reach the base of the two-hundred-foot summit pyramid, the wind has quit, the surrounding glaciers are gleaming in the cold sunlight, and Beckey's spirits seem to be picking up. Upon registering at the Marblemount ranger station the day before, the woman behind the desk had informed us that we would be the only people in the backcountry in the entire North Cascades National Park, a wilderness half the size of Delaware. Fred now drones on about this anomaly with mischievous delight, as if we have pulled a brilliant practical joke on the four million working stiffs who are currently going about their humdrum business in the cities and towns that sprawl two hours down the road from the trailhead parking lot.

The final pitch up Sahale—steep, downsloping rock slippery with frost—turns out to be trickier in these off-season conditions than any of us had anticipated. Beckey hogs the lead, and beetles his way up a razor-edged arête plastered with rime. When Mark and I join him on the tiny summit, he's manic, chattering, ebullient. Jagged granite ridges and avalanche-swept ice fields, some of the wildest country in the contermi-nous United States, extend into the distance in all directions, a concentration of mountains, in the words of the late William O. Douglas, "too numerous to count."

I wonder what's going through Fred's mind as he gazes off, silent now, at the glut of dizzying topography that surrounds us. Beckey has left his mark in many, many ranges, but nowhere more emphatically than here in the North Cascades. His life has been stitched into the very fabric of this remarkable landscape, wedded forever to a galaxy of peaks wearing names like Forbidden, Fury, the Dragon Teeth, Crooked Thumb, the Phantom, the Flagpole, Cutthroat, Despair. For several minutes he takes in the view; then he blinks a few times, his mental engine shifts visibly into a different gear, and a sly smile pierces the gray stubble sprouting from his face. "I don't know," Beckey declares, "I've never heard of anyone climbing Sahale in winter. This could be the first, I don't know, we might be the first comedy team to do it. The first winter ascent of Sahale, Jesus Christ, I don't know."

Like baseball fans analyzing the careers of Koufax or Mantle, climbers like to argue about which was Beckey's most amazing year. Some say it was 1946, when he pushed Alaskan mountaineering to a bold new plane by making the first ascent of an immense stone digit called the Devils Thumb. Others insist it was 1954, when he polished off Mount Deborah, Mount Hunter, and the Northwest Buttress of McKinley; or 1961, when Beckey teamed up with Chouinard to climb the West Face of South Howser Tower in the Canadian Bugaboos, a flying buttress of flawless white granite that is now widely regarded as the most beautiful alpine rock climb in North America; or 1963, when Beckey did forty-eight major routes, twenty-six of them first ascents.

When Beckey was on a roll, he would come down from the mountains only long enough to replace exhausted partners, which he went through like carpenters go through nails, and get the next weather forecast. His favorite way to do the latter, because it was free, was to dial up a long-distance operator in whatever Podunk burg happened to be near whatever mountain he wanted to climb next, and sweet-talk her into looking out the window and telling him if it was cloudy. Thanks to Beckey's unrelenting agenda, lining up partners and divining the weather in distant ranges required—and still requires—him to spend an inordinate amount of time in phone booths, often hours at a pop. A group of Beckey's partners once gave a slide show in which all the images were shots of the great alpinist, a receiver jammed to his ear, a paper bag full of change at the ready, yakking in pay phones from Fairbanks to Albuquerque. It had the audience rolling on the floor, howling with laughter.

As the summer of 1963 drew to a close, Fred was rock-climbing in eastern Oregon with Steve Marts and Eric Bjornstad. On the long drive back to Seattle, where they all lived, Beckey asked Bjornstad if he felt like doing another climb. "What do you have in mind?" Bjornstad inquired. "I can't tell you that," Beckey shot back, "but it's a big deal. It'll be worth your while." Accustomed to Beckey's paranoiac secrecy, Bjornstad agreed to the plan without pressing for more details, as did Marts, and the car sped past Seattle in the direction of Canada. "We drove through the night," Bjornstad remembers. "That was Fred's style. He'd never agree to stop and sleep; he always insisted on going directly from one project to another as quickly as possible. After we'd crossed the border into British Columbia and were almost into the mountains, Fred finally told me what it was: Slesse Mountain."

The unclimbed northeast buttress of Slesse jutted menacingly out of the Chilliwack Range twenty miles south of Hope, British Columbia. Beckey had been to the foot of the route twice before, a prow of smooth black diorite that soared more than a vertical half-mile from the forested valley. In 1956, a Trans-Canada Air Lines flight had slammed headlong into the face, imbedding the nose of the plane in the rock and killing all sixty-two passengers. The first time Beckey attempted the climb he found the base of the mountain to be "a maze of shattered metal, seat cushions, and fragmentary human remains." Despite the carnage, Beckey—ever the opportunist—was careful to keep an eye out for "any loose currency," as news bulletins had reported that one of the passengers had been carrying $80,000 in cash.

Neither of Beckey's first two attempts had gotten higher than halfway up the El Capitan–size buttress, and Bjornstad soon saw why. The climbing was devious and desperate. After two exhausting days on the wall, they still hadn't topped out, and nightfall caught them in the middle of a difficult pitch, forcing Marts to spend the night hanging in aid slings from a piton, shivering miserably. The weather held, though, and the following day, as Beckey later wrote, "A few more pitches, all broken and reasonable climbing, put us on the summit—very, very happy. The beauty queen of North Cascades routes had been done. . . . The length, exposure, and no-escape factors of this route will surely give it increasing fame as a great classic."

Slesse was in fact one of the finest climbs ever done in the United States, but only a handful of cognoscenti appreciated its significance or even knew of the peak. The ascent generated two sentences of minuscule type in *Sports Illustrated* that September, buried on a back page, where a postage-stamp-size picture of Beckey ran in the "Faces in the Crowd" column beneath a picture of a nurse from Brooklyn who'd landed a 94-pound tuna. A month after this forgettable blurb appeared, tens of millions of Americans saw a Seattle neighbor of Beckey's, Jim Whittaker, featured on the cover of *National Geographic* as the first American to reach the summit of Mount Everest. For a person as hypercompetitive as Beckey, the ubiquitous magazine must have been agonizing to look at.

The 1963 American Everest expedition was justly hailed as a whopping success, a triumph of national pride on the order of sending a man into space. While Beckey was eating cold beans from a can on mountain walls nobody had ever heard of, "Big Jim" Whittaker became a household name and rode the post-Everest hoopla all the way into the loftiest circles of Camelot itself, the Kennedy White House. A number of people wondered aloud why Beckey hadn't been part of the expedition, and wasn't now sharing in all the backslapping and hosannas.

Beckey's climbing record was more impressive than any of the Americans who had gone to Everest, and he had let it be known that he desperately wanted to be invited to Everest in 1963. But Norman Dyhrenfurth, the highly respected leader of the American expedition, was adamant that Beckey be kept off the team.

Although Beckey's skills as a mountaineer were unassailable, his cocky, impatient, notoriously unaccommodating personality had won him plenty of detractors. People whispered behind his back that he was dangerous to climb with, that he was ruthless to the point of recklessness in pursuit of summits. In 1947, Beckey had been on a Harvard expedition to Mount Asperity in British Columbia during which a team member had been killed in an avalanche. Another partner of Beckey's fell to his death in 1952 while they were attempting the North Face of Mount Baring in the North Cascades. In fact, neither of these accidents had anything to do with Beckey's actions or lack thereof, but they left a taint that clung to him like the smell of week-old fish.

The most serious blot on Beckey's good name occurred in the autumn of 1955, when he traveled to Nepal to attempt Lhotse—at the time the highest unclimbed mountain on earth—as part of a high-profile multinational expedition led by Dyhrenfurth. The post-monsoon weather was grim that fall, hammering the high Himalaya with gale after violent gale. Nevertheless, by October 22, two sherpas, Beckey, and a Swiss climber named Bruno Spirig were hunkered down in tents at 25,200 feet, poised to take a shot at the 27,890-foot summit.

The weather never let them. After two days of inconceivable cold and hurricane-force winds that tore the tents to ribbons, Dyhrenfurth got on the radio and ordered the team to descend. The four climbers managed to retreat to 24,200 feet, but at that point Spirig, who was suffering from snow blindness and altitude sickness, had a complete physical collapse. From a camp 3,000 feet lower, Dyhrenfurth watched through binoculars with growing alarm as Beckey left the incapacitated Swiss in a badly battered tent, without so much as a sleeping bag, and continued down with the sherpas through the ongoing storm. "None of us can understand this," a dismayed Dyhrenfurth wrote in his journal. "I decide to leave from here as early as possible tomorrow to get Spirig down, if he is still alive by then. We spend a worried and sleepless night."

Through a herculean effort, Dyhrenfurth and the rest of the team managed to climb up and rescue Spirig the following day, but Dyhrenfurth was livid at Beckey for abandoning his helpless partner and gave him a thorough chewing-out. Beckey insisted that at the time, muddled from hypoxia and extreme stress, he thought he was doing the right thing by leaving Spirig and going down to summon help. "You can't always act rationally on these trips," he explained to an Oregon newspaper reporter. "It's like guerrilla warfare up there." In any case, seven years after returning from Lhotse, when Beckey approached Dyhrenfurth about joining the American Everest expedition, Dyhrenfurth refused to even consider it.

"You can tell what really bothers Fred because that's the stuff he never mentions," says Sybil Goman, who has gotten as close to Beckey as perhaps a person can. Bjornstad concurs, adding that "Fred never mentioned his feelings about being excluded from the Everest trip, simply wouldn't talk about it, but it was obvious that it bothered him deeply. In 1962, when invitations were going out for the Everest team and it became clear Fred wasn't going to be included, he became very agitated and depressed. His response was to go out and do more climbing than ever." That year Beckey did thirty-three first ascents, a personal record.

People who know Beckey well speculate that even if the Lhotse climb hadn't turned ugly, he still wouldn't have been chosen for the Everest expedition, because it's simply not in Beckey's blood to be a team player. "What Fred wants to do," says his longtime friend Doug Stufflebeam, "Fred wants to goddamn *do*, right now, and he can't stand anyone telling him he can't."

"Dear old Fred, bless his heart, can be a very hard person to be around," explains Goman with a mix of affection and resignation. "Everyone will tell you that. That's one of the reasons he cycles through so many climbing partners. After a trip with Fred, they need to go off and cool down."

Beckey has never seemed to grasp the mundane social conventions on which the engines of civilization run; he's always been conspicuously out of step. "Fred is way off the chart," emphasizes Stufflebeam, who views Beckey as an oddball genius—a brilliant, if difficult, artist whose talent happens to be directed at vertical terrain rather than music or painting or mathematics. "Beckey's like an idiot savant," says Bjornstad. "He's amazing in the mountains, but he doesn't function very well in the world of people."

Beckey was a square peg right from the get-go. Born in Düsseldorf, Germany, in 1923—a tumultuous time in a troubled land—Beckey and his family immigrated to Seattle three years later. His mother was an accomplished opera singer, his father a physician described as a "cold fish." According to Goman, despite their new American surroundings, "Fred and his younger brother Helmy had a very German upbringing. Their mother dressed them in knickerbockers and sent them out into nature every morning to do breathing exercises."

The United States had just ended one war with Germany and would soon be fighting another. Young Wolfgang Friedrich Beckey—with his funny name, funny clothes, and immigrant parents—didn't have an easy time of it, growing up in that intensely xenophobic age. To put a lid on the schoolyard taunts, Beckey and his mother decided that thenceforth his name would be Fred.

From almost anywhere in Seattle, both the eastern and western horizons are dominated by the tantalizing profiles of high, craggy alps. Through the Boy Scouts, and later a local climbing club called the Mountaineers, Beckey was introduced to these rugged uplands as a teenager. Immediately and irrevocably, he fell under the mountains' thrall. It wasn't so much the tranquility of the wilderness that captivated him; his newfound obsession owed more to the fact that scrambling up dangerously steep ground was something he was uncannily good at, something that earned him the grudging respect, if not the affection, of his peers. It was a novel feeling, that respect, and he liked it. He liked it a lot.

In 1939, at the age of sixteen, Beckey made his inaugural first ascent: Mount Despair, an imposing pyramid of glacier-wrapped granite that is a prominent Cascade landmark. A rush of other first ascents soon followed. In 1942, in the company of his sixteen-year-old brother Helmy, Fred made the second ascent of Canada's remote Mount Waddington, one of the most fearsome mountains in North America at the time, a peak that had defeated sixteen attempts by strong climbers (one of whom died in a gruesome fall) and had succumbed only to a team led by the fabled Fritz Wiessner. When word of the Seattle teenagers' climb spread through the international climbing community, it was greeted initially with disbelief, then undiluted awe.

The ferocity of Fred Beckey's drive, his refusal to let anything keep him from the summits he desired, was already apparent by the time of the Waddington climb. And a dark side to that intensity was visible then as well. Published accounts of the expedition failed to note that there had been a third person along on the trip, a young climber named Eric Larsson. During the long trudge from sea level to the mountain, Larsson couldn't keep up with the Beckey brothers through the hideous Coast Range brush, and they refused to slow their blistering march to accommodate him. They ditched Larsson deep in the wilds of British Columbia, and continued on to Waddington by themselves. Left completely to his own devices, the abandoned climber reportedly managed to find his way back to civilization, although Beckey never bothered looking him up afterward to see how he fared.

In those days Beckey was so tightly wound, it probably never even crossed his mind that leaving Larsson behind was a crummy thing to do. I mean, Jesus Christ, they had a summit to reach, didn't they? What could be more important than that?

Beckey's unswerving focus, his burning hunger to climb, could blind him to the wishes of others. He was utterly oblivious to quirky personal habits that could drive his companions to the brink of violence. According to Bjornstad, for example, "Reading matter was always in short supply in climbing base camps, but whenever Fred would read a magazine, he'd tear out each page after he finished it, crumple it into a tight ball to exercise his forearms, then throw the page into the fire, even if nobody else had read it yet. A climber named Charlie Bell used to do the same thing, but he would at least put the pages to use by eating them, which cut down on food expenses."

Bjornstad recalls a trip he and Beckey made to New Mexico in 1965 to climb a new route on Shiprock. Three-quarters of the way up the sheer southwest buttress, the two climbers got into an epic shouting match, and Bjornstad told Beckey he was quitting the climb. They rappelled off the rock, and Bjornstad and his girlfriend, who had been waiting at base camp, walked out to the highway and began hitchhiking back to Seattle. Beckey, driving a pink 1956 Thunderbird, started back for Seattle a little while later to recruit a new partner, but refused to give Bjornstad a ride.

"Several times over the next few days we'd be standing on the highway shoulder with our thumbs out," Bjornstad remembers, "and Fred would cruise slowly by, taunting us, and then speed off down the road." By that point, the enmity between the two men was intense enough to sear exposed flesh; yet they were back climbing together later that same month. "Fred couldn't afford to stay mad at me for long," Bjornstad explains. "He was always needing partners, and I was one of the few people who could drop everything and go climbing with him in the middle of the week."

"Wha-wha-whaddaya call this stuff?" Beckey inquires of a woman with big hair and inch-long red fingernails as she hands out samples of pork sausage in an aisle of Thrifty Foods, a supermarket in Sedro Woolley, Washington. She forces a smile and launches into a spiel about the meat's myriad attributes, but she plainly doesn't know what to make of Beckey. Fresh out of the mountains, he's wearing a four-day growth of gray stubble, three tattered shirts, a decidedly gamy scent, and filthy pile pants that are sliding halfway down his bony ass. The woman can perhaps be excused for mistaking America's foremost alpinist for a wino who's wandered in from the street. "Ummm, ummm, not bad," Fred declares enthusiastically as he chews her product, "even if it does look like horse dick."

Beckey wolfs down six or seven more slices of sausage, then moves on to the seafood department, where he eats heartily from the sample tray of tempura, then to the deli counter, where they are handing out free tidbits of tortellini, and finally to the bakery, where the fare is chocolate-chip cookies and blueberry scones. "Saturdays are great in this supermarket," he says. "Not bad, yeah, yeah, pretty good food. I mean Jesus Christ, considering it's free and all." If Fred notices the scowls and wrinkled noses on the faces of the store employees as we systematically work our way down the aisles, he pays no heed whatsoever.

Beckey is still a master at subsisting on the cheap, at living off the fat of the land. And he continues to climb both relentlessly and with enviable skill: in the 1970s and 1980s, he traveled as far afield as Alaska, China, India, and Kenya in search of steep rock and ice; a year ago, he was leading poorly protected 5.10 face climbs in Yosemite. For seven decades Beckey has simply refused to grow old—he's sustained the restless energy and physical wherewithal of a badass adolescent through pure pigheaded determination.

But even orneriness has its limits. It's getting more and more obvious that Beckey is no longer a young man. His friends express growing concern about what will happen when Beckey's age finally catches up with him, as it eventually must. What will he do, they wonder, when his health fails and he's forced to forgo all the hustling and scamming? What will he do when he can no longer climb?

On a more practical level, there is also the question of how he will get by. Beckey clams up about his personal finances and employment history, even with his closest friends. In the past, he's been a sales rep, driven a truck, and worked the floor at Sears to support his climbing. During much of the 1960s, he promoted ski movies for John Jay and Dick Barrymore, and was apparently quite successful at it. But it's been many years now since anyone can remember Fred holding down a job. Lately his income, such as it is, is believed to come largely from slide shows and the royalties generated by his three-volume, thousand-page literary pièce de résistance: the *Cascade Alpine*

Guide, an obsessively researched guidebook detailing every climbing route on the 1,500 peaks that stud the convoluted crest of the Cascade Range in Washington State.

Whatever Beckey makes, nobody thinks it's enough to retire on. "I worry a lot about Fred winding up penniless on the street someday," Goman confesses. "For years now I've had this recurring nightmare, a very vivid one, in which Fred is in some asylum or shabby nursing home. In the dream, he's senile, completely out of it. I see him hunched over, frantically sorting paper clips, like a climber sorting hardware before a climb. And that's all he does, hour after hour, day after day: sort paper clips. Then I wake up with these incredible cold sweats. Fred and I split up a while ago, but that doesn't keep me from worrying about who's going to take care of the poor little spud when he gets too old to climb."

Beckey, Goman insists, has been "in extreme denial about his age for a long, long time." Indeed, for decades now he's been misrepresenting his age in published accounts of his climbs; well into his forties, he was still claiming to be thirty-three. But Goman believes the years at long last are beginning to reel him in. Lately Beckey has failed on climbs that he would have cruised up just five years ago, and young partners have increasingly had to stop in mid-ascent and wait for the legendary alpinist to catch his breath.

"I think Fred is finally starting to feel his mortality," Goman asserts. "His activity level has dropped by an order of magnitude over the last few years. Because he's less active, I also think Fred is feeling his loneliness for the first time. He's always been gregarious, he's passed through a lot of people's lives, but he's never really been emotionally engaged. Now he's paying the price. If you look beneath the surface, you'll find that Fred is a very lonely man."

———

If it's difficult to comprehend how Beckey has done what he's done on the heights, it's not hard to understand why. To climb a virgin peak—to know you're the first soul since time immemorial to stand atop a landmark as ponderable as a mountain's summit—confers satisfactions on the alpine pioneer that are many and lasting. Not least among them is the traditional right of the first-ascensionist to name the mountain he has climbed.

Beckey, it goes without saying, has christened many, many peaks. Somewhat surprisingly, only once did he ever name a mountain after a woman. The recipient of the honor was said to be brilliant, beautiful, strong-willed, athletic. Of Greek heritage, she was fluent in several languages and reportedly smoked cigars with panache. Her name was Vasiliki. Beckey met her skiing at Stevens Pass in the winter of 1952, when he was just twenty-nine. They went skiing a few more times, played tennis together, attended a party or two. By June, though, Vasiliki had met somebody else, a high-powered lawyer who would one day become a public figure appointed by President Reagan to federal district court; she married the lawyer a few months later, and Vasiliki's romance with Beckey was over before it had really even begun.

Aflame with unrequited love, in the summer of 1952, Beckey hiked into the North Cascades and established a base camp beneath a massif of sharply hewn rock pinnacles near the eastern margin of the range. The most alluring of these spires adorned the crest of a towering granite knife-edge that soon thereafter appeared on USGS maps as Vasiliki Ridge.

If Vasiliki broke Beckey's heart, he appeared to get over her in short order. Beckey was a contemporary of Hugh Hefner's, and he took the Playboy Philosophy as the gospel. He flaunted his independence by dating a multitude of women, committing himself to none. There was the airline stewardess, the topless showgirl, the real estate agent, the geologist, the trapeze artist from Tarzana . . . the list goes on and on. "Fred was from the old school," Goman says. "He liked to be seen with wild and flashy women, it was a status thing. He had a girl in every port, and many of them were absolute bombshells."

Beckey has often opined—loudly and at great length—that marriage is for fools, that it's one of the worst things a climber can do. I was thus taken aback one night, lying in the wind-whipped tent beneath Sahale Peak, when he confessed that he'd actually come close to tying the knot. When I asked why he hadn't, Fred replied, "I don't know, I probably should have."

"Who was the woman?"

"What makes you think there was just one?"

"Was it the woman you named that ridge after back in the 1950s? Are you sorry you didn't settle down with Vasiliki?" I pressed.

"Whaddaya think the weather's doing outside?" Beckey fired back. "Anything movin' in from the southwest?" It was clear that the conversation was over. For several minutes, all was silent except for the rasp of the wind. Then, from the far side of the tent, Fred spoke again. "Yeah, that Vasiliki was quite a gal," he declared in a soft voice freighted with regret. "Jesus Christ, she was really something." A moment later, he rolled over and began to snore.

As it happens, several of Beckey's friends report that recently he's been talking a lot about marriage. Apparently, he's even been looking for a nine-to-five job, and has spoken to a realtor about buying an inexpensive house. Everyone remarks how much Fred has mellowed over the past few years. So perhaps Beckey's tenure as an incorrigible climbing bum really is coming to an end. Maybe the aging gypsy is finally ready to hang up his ice ax. But then again, maybe not.

Beckey, Mark Bebie, and I are bumping along a rutted dirt road deep in the heart of the North Cascades. Fred is yammering on about tentative plans he has to visit the Himalaya, to climb in Patagonia, to go back to Alaska to attempt the Mooses Tooth. We round a bend, and far above the road, a striking granite buttress comes into view, rising steep and clean for a thousand feet or more.

"Hey, Fred!" Mark exclaims. "Check that out! Any routes been done on that wall?"

"No, nobody's been up there. Decent rock, I don't know, yeah, probably real solid granite. Climbers today, all they want to do is go to the gym, Jesus Christ, nobody's been up there. Memorial Day, I don't know, the approach will be free of snow by then, might be a good time to put up a route on it."

"Screw that," Mark says, pulling to a stop to get a better view of the unclimbed face. "That buttress looks so great I think I'll head up there next weekend, while you're in Chicago giving that slide show."

Beckey glares at Bebie, his eyes flashing. "You ever had a broken leg, Mark?" he asks. Bebie turns and looks hard at Beckey, trying to gauge the seriousness of the threat. *He's just kidding around*, Bebie thinks. *The old buzzard wouldn't really come after me if I stole the route. Or would he?* Beckey stares back, matching Bebie's gaze without the slightest hint of a smile.

Bebie blinks first. He turns away and resumes driving out of the mountains. "Don't worry yourself, Fred," he says with a nervous little laugh. "You know I'd never steal one of your lines. The route's all yours, old dad. The route's all yours."

Author's Note: Fred Beckey passed away on October 30, 2017. He was ninety-four years old.

EMBRACE THE MISERY

*The world is going to hell. But that's no reason
to get your panties in a wad.*

You are by nature an optimist, a happy idiot. No personal
disaster or run of bad luck has ever shaken your faith that the
march of time brings progress. You believe the wicked eventually get their due. You're confident that truth will come to
light. You've never doubted that a hundred years hence, the
world will be a better place.

Until lately. Lately you've found yourself wondering if the
end of civilization might be at hand, and you are not alone
in your apprehension. Pessimism drifts in the air like a viru-
lent pathogen, infecting multitudes. The media deliver daily
reports of contemptible politicians and enraged mobs, religious fanatics and failed states, widespread unemployment
and ecological catastrophe. A friend has been goading you to
buy a gun and plenty of ammunition "before it's too late." (He
owns more than thirty weapons himself: shotguns, hunting
rifles, semiautomatic assault rifles, and an astonishing variety
of handguns.) However you parse it, the future looks increasingly grim and Malthusian.

What happened? How did this collective despair displace
the easy confidence of recent memory?

The technological miracles of our enlightened age were
supposed to banish ignorance and alleviate human suffering.
It was only a few decades ago that the Berlin Wall came down,

THIS ESSAY WAS PRESENTED AS A LECTURE ON JULY 16, 2010, AT *LA MILANESIANA*, THE ITALIAN
ARTS AND CULTURE FESTIVAL.

prompting Francis Fukuyama to announce the triumph of Western ideals over the forces of tyranny, and proclaim that war had become obsolete.

"What we may be witnessing," Fukuyama famously gushed, "is not just the end of the Cold War . . . but the end of history as such: that is, the end point of mankind's ideological evolution."

What happened, say Fukuyama's detractors, is that his giddy post-historical prophecy failed to account for the second law of thermodynamics—the scientific principle that explains why an ice cube melts when placed in hot espresso, and why you can remember the past but can't foresee the future. Reduced to its essence, the second law ordains that entropy increases over time. Or to put it another way, deterioration, disarray, and disintegration are written into the cosmic bargain. Things fall apart; the center cannot hold. Progress inevitably leads to annihilation. It's the supreme paradox.

According to the second law of thermodynamics, the earth is destined to become a frozen wasteland, devoid of life—an outcome that's beyond dispute.

The end of the world isn't slated to occur any time soon, however. Although the entropy of the cosmos is irreversibly on the rise, the entropy of its constituent systems fluctuates up and down at varying rates. Incongruously, disorder retreats in some provinces of the firmament even as it relentlessly advances in aggregate.

Rain occasionally falls on the Sahara. Mothers give birth amid the devastation of earthquakes and war zones. Empires rise, fall, and are superseded by new empires. The second law of thermodynamics decrees that ice cubes will melt in your espresso, but the freezer in your kitchen will create new ice cubes as long as it's drawing energy from an outside source (thereby boosting the entropy in some other corner of existence). The second law of thermodynamics, in other words, does not stipulate a nonstop slide into the abyss. The ride down is likely to be unhurried, and interrupted by any number of uplifting diversions. The final unsparing destination probably won't be reached until long after your charmed life has run its course.

Which doesn't mean your current angst should be dismissed as unwarranted paranoia. Most people in your privileged Western milieu have spent their entire lives inside a bubble of peace and prosperity, but to believe "la dolce vita" will continue forever is delusional. Sooner or later, the party always ends. Every great civilization since antiquity has gone into decline, and you can't really pin the blame on entropy. The fault, dear Brutus, is not in the second law of thermodynamics, but in ourselves.

Ordinary human behavior has proven to be more than sufficient impetus for war, economic collapse, and myriad other far-reaching calamities. Accordingly, nobody should be surprised if one of history's recurring periods of adversity turns out to be coming in for a landing, and it would be naive to presume that such a downturn, whenever it arrives, will be brief. The era christened the Dark Ages by Francesco Petrarca (commonly Anglicized as Petrarch) afflicted Europe from the Fall of Rome until the Renaissance, a span of some nine hundred years. For all anyone knows, we might be witnessing the onset of a similarly protracted spell of gloom.

Predicting the future is a fool's errand, of course. But whatever lies ahead, you can take some comfort in the weedy resilience of our species. If the world is in fact teetering on the brink of a new Dark Age, *Homo sapiens* will not lack strategies for coping. Many people, for instance, turn to religion during difficult times—although personally, you happen to find literature more effective than scripture. When prospects grow dire, you derive courage and reassurance from writers as disparate as Thucydides, Walter Bonatti, Annie Proulx, and Cormac McCarthy. If the going gets especially tough, you consult Albert Camus.

———

In his book-length essay *The Myth of Sisyphus*, Camus reinterprets the legend of the eponymous protagonist, for whom the gods concoct an infernal torture: Sisyphus must push an immense rock to the top of a mountain, only to have it tumble back to the depths of hell every time he approaches the summit, compelling him to return to the bottom and roll the rock uphill again. And again. And again. The gods, Camus explains, are convinced there is "no more dreadful punishment than futile and hopeless labor." Each time Sisyphus trudges down to roll the rock back up the slope, his "boundless grief is too heavy to bear."

Be that as it may, when Sisyphus manages to wrap his mind around the inescapability of his predicament and takes responsibility for it, he finds himself liberated from his torment. He thereby subverts the twisted pleasure that the gods derive from inflicting "futile sufferings" and makes himself master of his own destiny, even as he continues to push the boulder up the mountain for eternity.

Sisyphus determines that "all is well," despite the ceaseless misery he must endure. "The struggle itself toward the heights is enough to fill a man's heart," Camus observes. "One must imagine Sisyphus happy."

As a gray-haired alpinist, you've spent more than half a century struggling on high escarpments, inventing purpose out of hardship, and conjuring meaning from otherwise senseless acts. For Sisyphus to be contented as he toils beneath his rock doesn't strike you as far-fetched.

But when you contemplate the uncertain future and the Sisyphean tribulations it's apt to impose, actual joy seems a little too much to hope for. All things considered, you'd settle for stoical resolve.

ACKNOWLEDGMENTS

I'm grateful to the editors at the publications where these pieces first appeared: Mark Bryant, John Rasmus, Laura Hohnhold, Lisa Chase, Larry Burke, Kiki Yablon, Brad Wetzler, Katie Arnold, Sue Casey, and Hampton Sides at *Outside*; Jack Wiley, Jim Doherty, Don Moser, Caroline Despard, Ed Rich, Connie Bond, Judy Harkison, Bruce Hathaway, Tim Foote, and Frances Glennon at *Smithsonian*; Phil Zaleski and David Abramson at *New Age Journal*; David Remnick and Sasha Weiss at *The New Yorker*; and Kate Lee at *Medium*.

At Penguin Random House, I'm indebted to LuAnn Walther, Bill Thomas, Kate Runde, Catherine Tung, Alison Rich, Kathy Trager, Rose Courteau, Bette Alexander, Andy Hughes, Kathy Hourigan, Maria Carella, John Fontana, John Pitts, Suzanne Herz, Beth Meister, Janet Cooke, Sonny Mehta, Carol Janeway, Thomas Dobrowolski, Deb Foley, Rebecca Gardner, Jenna Ciongoli, Laura Swerdloff, Amy Metsch, Anne Messitte, Dana Maxson, Russell Perreault, John Siciliano, Marty Asher, Bonnie Thompson, Anke Steinecke, Laura Golden, Bill Shannon, Nancy Rich, Joelle Dieu, Serena Lehman, and Pauline James.

For providing advice, support, opportunity, and inspiration over the years, I owe special thanks to Linda Moore, Becky Hall, Bill Briggs, Chhongba Sherpa, Tom Hornbein, Kathy Hornbein, Shannon Costello, David Roberts, Sharon Roberts, Ed Ward, Laura Brown, Pam Brown, Helen Apthorp, Roman Dial, Peggy Dial, Matt Hale, Tom Sam Steed, Sam Brower,

Deborah Shaw, Nick Miller, Conrad Anker, Jimmy Chin, Steve Rottler, Carine McCandless, Marie Tillman, Trisha Dittrick, Elizabeth O'Herrin Lee, Michelle D'Arcy, Doug Chabot, Genevieve Walsh, David Quammen, Barry Lopez, Dan Stone, Charley Mace, Josh Jespersen, Geoff Friefeld, Carol Friefeld, David Turner, Rick Accomazzo, Gerry Accomazzo, Bob Kauffman, Greg Davis, Ted Callahan, Steve Kroft, Andy Court, Beth Bennett, Tom Davies, Marc Twight, Mark Fagan, Sheila Cooley, Dave Jones, Chris Gulick, Yvon Chouinard, Lou Dawson, Barbara Hirschbichler, Nate Zinsser, Larry Bruce, Molly Higgins, Holly Crary, Mark Rademacher, Mugs Stump, Kitty Calhoun, Colin Grissom, Steve Swenson, Dale Remsberg, Jim Balog, Chip Lee, Pete Athans, Dan Cauthorn, Klev Schoening, Kasha Rigby, Phil Henderson, Jacqui Edgerly, Ralph Backstrom, KT Miller, Ryan Hudson, Jeremy Jones, Robin Hill, Brody Leven, Christian Somoza, Neal Beidleman, Amy Beidleman, Ron Harris, Mary Harris, Sally La Venture, Mike Pilling, Kerry Kirkpatrick, John Winsor, Harry Kent, Owen Kent, René Archambault, Mark Donahue, Quinn Brett, Ruth Fecych, David Rosenthal, Charlie Conrad, Jonathan Southard, Bill Meyer, Mike Meloy, Masood Ahmad, Erica Stone, Richard Blum, Tshering Dorje, Aruna Uprety, Greg Child, Chris Reveley, Steve Komito, Chris Wejchert, Monty McCutcheon, Joe Veltre, Ray Meyers, Craig Brown, Denny Sedlack, Dan Janosko, Eric Ackerman, Scott Van Dyke, Eric Zacharias, Carolyn Fronczak, Kevin Cuevas, Lance Richards, Coco Dughi, Jeremy Rodgers, Ania Mohelicki, Sean Penn, Eddie Vedder, Amy Berg, Chris Conway, Jann Wenner, Randy Mankin, Seymour Hersh, Erica Huggins, Lance Black, Jenni Lowe-Anker, Steve Gipe, Pamela Hainsworth, Betsy Quammen, Renan Ozturk, Chai Vasarhelyi, Mike Alkaitis, Cecilia Perucci, Roberto Santachiara, Brian Nuttall, Christine Durnan, Drew Simon, Alexandra Martella, Julie Martinez, David Wolf, Eric Love, Josie Heath, Margaret Katz, Karin Krakauer, Wendy

Krakauer, Sarah Krakauer, Andrew Krakauer, Bill Costello, Tim Stewart, Robin Krakauer, Rosie Lingo, Ali Stewart, Maureen Costello, Ari Kohn, Miriam Kohn, Kelsi Krakauer, A. J. Krakauer, Devin Lingo, Zay Lingo, Abilene Rose Lingo, Murphy Lingo, Nick Jenkins, and Estelle Jenkins.